Dolls' House
Soft Furnishings

DOLLS' HOUSE
SOFT FURNISHINGS
IN ¹⁄₁₂ SCALE

❋

NICK AND ESTHER FORDER

David & Charles

CONTENTS

INTRODUCTION

Today's dedicated dolls' house miniaturists wish to achieve ever higher and higher standards in the quality of their work. While woodwork, wallpaper, furniture and accessories all look highly realistic it is often the unconvincing soft furnishings which let the whole thing down. This book addresses this problem and advises on convincing soft furnishings which can be achieved by anyone from the advanced needleworker to the complete novice with ideas, designs, patterns and instructions to suit individual talents. So whether you are comfortable working with glue, needle and thread or embroidery canvas there are plenty of ideas tailor made for you and every one designed to give a splendid, professional result.

Most of us try to establish a date at which to set our miniature scenes and for this reason our book is divided into seven different periods, with soft furnishing projects relating to each one.

Tudor & Stuart Style Our first chapter deals with soft furnishings used from about 1485-1714 – the Tudor and Stuart period. Before this fabrics were not employed with any great variety in the home although wools, linens, cottons and silk fibres were available. During the Tudor and Stuart period different fabrics began to be used more widely and efficiently within the home with rugs, curtains and decorative bedding and eventually completely or partially upholstered chairs becoming standard. In this chapter we examine various ways of producing items which may have been used at the time – bed drapes and coverlets, wall hangings, pillows, cushions, curtains and various table coverings.

Georgian Style In the eighteenth century elegant fabric window dressings were established as the norm and upholstered furniture in a number of styles was more and more widely adopted. There was an increase in the production of woollen carpets both at home and abroad which were in demand despite their expense, as was linen cloth for

Gothic villa containing several of our miniature room sets.

bedding, table covers and linings. Our second chapter deals with the styles of the Georgian period and shows a number of soft furnishings relating to the times including a swagged window dressing, embroidered pole screens and a complete bed treatment.

Regency Style The period from about 1790 to 1830, known as Regency, saw the awakening of the notion of interior decoration. It was a time when soft furnishings came into their own. In this chapter we look at styles of carpets, curtains, upholstered furniture and pole screens, all interpreted in miniature.

Victorian Style The period from 1830 to 1900 is described in chapter 4. Examples of furnishings are taken from styles varying from the ornate high Victorian 1850s to the comparatively simple look of the Arts and Crafts movements of the late 1800s at the end of the period. During this time no room would be complete without its embroidered sampler and we also include instructions on making a sofa, bell pull, curtains, carpets, a bedspread and more.

Early Twentieth Century New inventions and materials produced marked changes in interiors between 1901 and the 1940s which are described in our next chapter. It features three room sets: an Edwardian nursery, a 1930s living room and a bedroom furnished with a flavour of 1950s Hollywood, complete with soft furnishings including a rag rug, quilts, carpets and even a lamp shade.

Contemporary Living Some dolls' house enthusiasts are interested in modern interiors so we have a chapter which looks at developing ideas from the 1970s until the present day. It includes designs for use in bedrooms, bathrooms and living areas with a highly modern living space epitomising the beginning of the twenty-first century. Find out how to make tea towels for ½ scale, towels and a shower curtain plus a table for a conservatory among other projects.

Design Classics Our final selection looks at what might be termed design classics: styles which have become a standard and never really look out of date. Although the miniature rooms created in these styles are close representations of originals, soft furnishings taken from them can look at home in any contemporary setting. We chose the American Colonial look, Larsson style and the Shaker style.

Do not feel you have to use the ideas shown in this book exactly as we have because nearly all the soft furnishings in each chapter can be adapted to suit your own requirements. We have shown them in authentically styled rooms with the intention that they should inspire.

If, when you read this book, you have not yet decided on the period in which you wish to set your dolls' house or individual room, perhaps our pictures will help. However, if you already possess the dolls' house or room box be aware that its period styling and proportions may well dictate what you should do. It is always possible to create a setting later than that of the room or dolls' house but it should never be earlier. We have done this with our twentieth-century living room which is located in a late eighteenth-century Gothic villa and has been furnished in the style of the 1930s. After all, life always moves on. Similarly, a room of any period can contain furniture and objects of a previous time but not from the future. Furnishing rooms within a dolls' house is perhaps what most of us still try to do. For that reason a number of our miniature rooms have been incorporated into our Gothic villa. Each of our room settings is as pure in style as possible in order to avoid confusion.

Once the important time frame has been decided upon the fun can begin. It can help to imagine the person or family who lives within the space to help set social standing or personal taste and the acquisition of a figure or two might even begin to add personality to the setting. Try to imagine how a room might be used and visualise how people might move about within it. Think what colours were used in the period and which are most applicable to the kind of setting you wish to create. Piece by piece a picture of the room will develop and very quickly the items needed to decorate and furnish that room will become apparent. Most of all, however, remember that working on miniatures should be fun and a reflection of that fun in a setting is no bad thing.

During the Regency period soft furnishings became more important than ever before. Colours were more daring and people took a great interest in Greek and Roman styles and in Oriental items. This Chinese style Morning Room (see page 62) would have been a favourite with the Prince Regent who incorporated chinoiserie styles in his great Pavilion at Brighton.

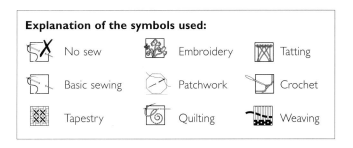

Explanation of the symbols used:

No sew	Embroidery	Tatting
Basic sewing	Patchwork	Crochet
Tapestry	Quilting	Weaving

TUDORS & STUARTS

THIS LONG PERIOD FROM 1485 to 1714 encompasses a move towards the establishment of a settled and comfortable home. Prior to the latter part of the fifteenth or early sixteenth centuries life for noble or wealthy families was often unsettled as they moved from place to place, often carrying their possessions with them. Tapestries in the form of wall hangings, embroidered cushions and various decorative coverings and draperies were easy to transport and could readily be put to use to provide warmth and comfort wherever home might be established. But as the period progressed life became more settled and soft furnishings expanded to include more lavish bedding, carpets, rugs and upholstered chairs.

At the start of this period the limited soft furnishings were in silks, rich velvets, brocades and damasks, usually in bright, warm colours. Countries specialised in a specific material or finish. Italy and France exported patterned velvets and fine silks, for example, England and Spain produced woollen cloths and Flanders concentrated first on woollen weaving and then on fine linen damasks. England and then the low countries and Florence were famed for their embroidered tapestries of silk and wool with gold threads worked on a velvet or linen background. These would depict scenes or tales of daily life or legend and were popular among the wealthy across Europe. However, for most people plain linen or woollen textiles were most commonly employed for clothing and domestic use alike, being both less costly and more readily available.

By the sixteenth century England was at peace, enabling life to become more secure. The middle classes began to establish themselves, building houses more as homes and less as fortresses. Windows, now glazed, could be large, permitting sunlight to illuminate the home. More permanent housing meant greater attention could be paid to decorative detail, particularly soft furnishings, while the new larger windows permitted experimental window treatments. The upholstered chair made its debut and tablecloths and covers added further comfort.

It was the bed which probably received the greatest attention at this time, becoming the most significant piece of furniture in the home. For the wealthy it was a large canopied affair with elaborate carvings and fanciful trimmings. It was draped with rich bed hangings which could be drawn round to exclude draughts and provide privacy. Even more modest homes would have such a bed but usually with drapes of wool or linen – privacy was important because in most cases a bedroom would be shared or double as a corridor.

The seventeenth century saw greater advancement in fabric production together with a wider demand for soft

furnishings. Crewelwork, petite point, bobbin lace and raised embroidery all became popular and fashionable and at the same time the manufacture of woven and embroidered wool carpets was introduced to Europe on a large scale. Overall the sixteenth and seventeenth centuries experienced greater advancement towards the creation of a comfortable home than had probably been seen during the previous fifteen hundred years.

❋

ELIZABETHAN BEDROOM

This bedroom, shown above, would date from somewhere between 1580 and 1600 and might form part of a middle-class home as the upper part of the wall and ceiling are plain – the ceiling of a more noble household would have

This typical Elizabethan bedroom is dominated by the poster bed, complete with drapes and matching cover. The panels and rebated strips are provided by Tom Burchmore, the magnificent bed is by Barbara Moore of Pear Tree Miniatures and the other furniture is by craftsman David Hurley. Flowers are by Gill Rawling of Petite Fleur (see page 166).

been higher and feature ornate plaster decoration. Nevertheless, the walls are of linenfold wood panels which we have given a light colour in accordance with the style of the day. The floor is also of wood in the form of boarding which we stained to a darker colour. There is also a fireplace with brick back and stone floor built into the room with firedogs which support logs for burning.

The room has been furnished simply with an ambry, chest, cradle and chair with linenfold design back but the most significant piece of furniture is the carved oak bed which we have fitted with complete soft furnishings from the mattress to the bed drapes and cover. Accessories are few but here include candlesticks, a stonework jug with silver mounts and a pewter jug containing examples of an early rose.

For this setting we made the bed hangings, coverlet and pillow from antique cotton velvets, a cushion for the chest from a piece of Victorian velvet, a cover for the top of the ambry, a wall hanging, leather chair seat and woven rush mat for the floor. We also made mattresses and bed sheets plus an alternative set of embroidered bedding for a more feminine setting.

THE BED

During this period beds were enclosed with elaborately embroidered hangings and curtains both for privacy and warmth. Such bed coverings were considered of great value and bed covers, pillows and mattresses have been recorded in wills as items worthy enough to be bequeathed to friends and relations.

Mattresses for Tudor and Elizabethan beds were made from a variety of materials. Beds for wealthy households had layers of mattresses piled upon the bed boards or strips of leather stretched across the frame. Straw pallets were used at one time to make the bed board or leather strips more comfortable and it has been recorded that logs were used for head rests. Eventually wool and feather mattresses replaced the straw pallet. A stuffed woollen mattress was first placed on top of the boards or leather strips and then a feather mattress on top of this.

Enormous linen sheets were laid over the mattresses and these were so large and difficult to launder that they often remained unwashed for months on end, particularly if the weather was bad. Bed coverings were highly prized but not plentiful and women often lent each other their lying-in sheets with apologies for their uncleanliness. On top of the sheets housewives placed fustian or wool blankets, feather and down pillows and a coverlet. Pillows were encased in embroidered pillow beres measuring 35 x 12in.

PLEATED BED DRAPES

Old fabrics are ideal for soft furnishings in an historical setting because they give an aged look which cannot be achieved with new materials. For the bed drapes and cover with matching pillow bere we used a wonderful piece of old cotton velvet fabric. Similarly, a piece of cotton velvet

salvaged from an old pieced patchwork was fashioned into the mauve cushion on the chest at the foot of the bed. However, note that velvet is difficult to embroider and you may prefer to use evenweave fabric for the embroidered cover and pillow bere. (For an alternative bedding set with a more feminine look see also page 15.)

To make these drapes you will need paper for a pattern, cotton velvet, lining fabric, thread, a Pretty Pleater, glue, suitable fringe or braid and ribbon or thin card. If you do not wish to do any sewing, follow the technique used for the curtains in the Regency dining room (page 56) where the hems are bonded with fusible webbing (Bondaweb). Use additional webbing to bond the curtain to the lining.

First cut a paper pattern 7 x 7¼in for the side drapes and 4¾ x 7¼in for the end panels. These measurements include a ½in seam allowance. Lay out your lining fabric, pin the paper patterns on top and cut four side drapes and two end panels. Repeat to cut the same number of pieces from your main fabric.

Remove the patterns and pin a lining to each fabric piece with right sides facing. Machine stitch all round, taking a ½in seam allowance and working two diagonal stitches across each corner; leave a gap for turning. Cut the seam allowances on the diagonal at each corner and trim the seam allowances to ¼in, leaving a wedge-shaped lip at the gap. (If you trim the seam at the gap it is fiddly trying to turn it in later.) Turn right sides out and use a soft, blunt-ended tool to push out the corners. Tuck in the seam allowances at the gap and slipstitch closed. Press each panel, placing it between cotton pressing cloths first to avoid squashing the pile. Now attach a fringe or suitable braid to the bottom edge of each drapery panel with slipstitch or blind herringbone stitch (see page 160). Pleat each drape in the Pretty Pleater (see page 161). Finally, glue or sew a ribbon or thin card across the top of each pleated drape and glue it securely to the inside of the bed frame (see picture on page 10).

EMBROIDERED BED COVER

This bed cover was made from the same cotton velvet and lining fabric as the drapes but you can use an evenweave fabric if preferred which is easier to embroider. To make it you will need paper for a pattern, cotton velvet (or evenweave fabric), lining fabric, tailor's chalk, embroidery cottons in the colours of your choice and a suitable needle. If you are not confident about your embroidery

add seam allowance

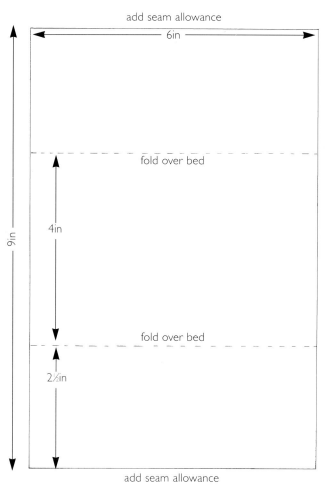

Fig. 1 Elizabethan Bed Cover Pattern

skills simply omit the embroidery or use a decorative fabric instead.

First measure the width of the bed and the side drop and then prepare a paper pattern. Our bed was 6 x 4in with a 2½in drop so our pattern was 6in long and 9in wide (2½ + 4in + 2½). Add ½in seam allowances all round. Pin your pattern to the cotton velvet and cut out the pattern. Repeat to cut out the lining. The design used for our bed cover is a simple one of flowers, leaves and vines (see below). Use this or devise your own pattern. This design is meant to go on the top of the bed only but you can embroider the sides too, if desired. If so, note how the pattern will run when the cover is in place.

Fig. 2 Bed Cover Design

It is difficult to transfer patterns onto velvet. You may be able to re-create the pattern by stitching the vines and stems at random on the fabric. Then stitch flower heads and leaves where appropriate. Alternatively, use a tailor's chalk pencil, sharpened to a fine point, to draw the pattern onto the velvet. If you are using an evenweave linen you may wish to transfer the pattern using one of the methods given on page 156.

Mount the main fabric in a frame, if desired, (see pages 156-157) and embroider the design, choosing whichever stitches and colours you like. For the stems choose an outline stitch such as stem stitch or backstitch; for the flowers try satin, lazy daisy or straight stitches and use French knots for the flower centres (see page 158 for details on working embroidery stitches.)

When the embroidery work is finished pin the cover to the lining fabric with right sides facing. Machine stitch all round, taking a ½in seam allowance. Stitch the corners and trim the seams to ¼in in the same way as for the bed drapes. Turn right sides out and use a soft, blunt-ended tool to push out the corners. Tuck in the seam allowances at the gap and close with blind herringbone stitch or slipstitch. Place the bed cover between pressing cloths and press, then place the finished bed cover on the bed.

EMBROIDERED PILLOW BERE

Make the splendid matching pillow bere from fabrics and embroidery cottons left over from the bed cover. You will also need paper and rice or salt for the stuffing.

For a standard bed 4in wide first cut a paper pattern 4¼ x 1¾in. Pin it to your fabric and cut out. Repeat to cut the pattern from lining. Mount the main fabric in a frame, if desired, (see pages 156-157) and embroider it following the same design as on the bed cover. Once the embroidery is complete sew the two pillow fabric pieces together with right sides facing, taking a ½in seam allowance and leaving a gap to turn through. Trim the seam allowances as before, turn and fill with rice or salt then stitch the gap closed with blind herringbone stitch or slipstitch.

STRAW PALLET

At one time straw pallets were used to make the bed more comfortable and were laid on top of leather strips or boards in the bed frame. To give the bed a proper shape under the cover you will need to make either the straw pallet or a

pair of mattresses (see below). This straw pallet is suitable for a large tester bed (four-poster) or a truckle bed (a low bed on wheels stored under a larger bed for use by a servant). To make it all you need is some raffia (available from craft shops, some gift shops or garden shops), some dried grasses and herbs and matching thread or white fabric glue. Simply plait (braid) raffia strings mixed with the dried grasses and herbs into 6in lengths. Sew these together with matching cotton to the correct width of the bed or glue them together with thin white fabric glue.

WOOL AND FEATHER MATTRESSES

Straw pallets were eventually replaced by a woollen mattress topped with a feather one – the woollen mattress acted rather like today's sprung bed bases. Start by making the woollen mattress using horsehair fabric for the cover and sheep's wool for the stuffing. Horsehair fabric is normally used as an interfacing for tailoring and can be found in dressmaking suppliers. Processed and washed sheep's wool is readily available from craft shops but you may prefer to collect wool from fences, gorse bushes or sheep farms while on a country walk. For the feather mattress to go on top use unbleached cotton for the cover and fine down feathers for the stuffing.

For each mattress cut two pieces of horsehair/cotton fabric 1in larger in each dimension than the size required – in this case, 7 x 5in. Pin the pieces together with right sides facing and hand or machine stitch the sides and ends, taking a ½in seam allowance and leaving a small gap for turning and filling. Make one or two diagonal stitches across the corners in the same way as for the bed drapes. Trim the seam allowances to ¼in except at the gap where the seam allowance should remain untrimmed. Turn the cover right sides out. Use a soft, blunt-ended tool to push out the corners and press the seams with a steam iron. Generously fill the cover with sheep's wool or feathers to make the mattress look ample and comfortable. Pin the gap and stitch closed with slipstitch or blind herringbone stitch.

BED SHEETS

For authenticity you may like to make bed sheets even though these will not be seen under the bed cover in this setting. You will need evenweave linen fabric and fine matching thread (see page 154).

For the bottom sheet cut a 7¾ x 10½in rectangle of fabric. Machine stitch ⅜in from the edge on all four edges then fold the corners under on the diagonal to make a mitred corner. Trim off the excess at the corner, as shown. Turn all four edges over along the stitch line and press with a steam iron. Pin the raw edges under and hem with blind herringbone stitch. Press the finished sheet and use it to cover the mattresses.

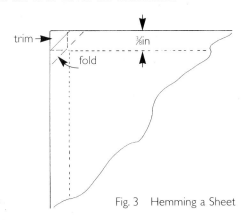

Fig. 3   Hemming a Sheet

To make the enormous top sheet cut a 10½ x 11½in rectangle of evenweave fabric. Machine stitch ½in from the edge on all four sides. Press under the edges along the stitch line with a steam iron in the same way as for the bottom sheet. At the corners fold the fabric on the diagonal and trim the excess as before. Pin the raw edges under and hem with blind herringbone stitch. Press the sheet and place on the bed.

ALTERNATIVE FLORAL BEDDING SET

Since the bed is the most important piece of furniture in the Elizabethan bedroom it sets the tone for all the decorations. If you wish to create a room set with a very feminine feel then the bed hangings, valance and bed cover shown on page 18 make a good starting point.

FLORAL BED DRAPES

These drapes are made to fit around the posts of a bed about 6¼ x 4 x 7¾in. The height or dimensions of the curtains can be varied by omitting some of the flowers and border. If you prefer the curtains to hang inside the bed frame, make four the size of the smaller curtains given here, and two using just the narrow end of the large hangings. Notice that in this design each flower is slightly different, the colours vary and the position of the flowers changes on each hanging. This was perfectly normal during the Tudor period. Vary the colours to suit your planned room scheme and feel free to reduce or extend the number of colours used. This design may also be adapted to make a wall hanging.

To make the drapes you will need about 10in of black silk satin fabric (this is sufficient to make the matching valances and bed cover too), unbleached calico for linings, DMC stranded embroidery cotton in the colours listed in the key (see page 17), white dressmakers' tracing paper, 35 x ¼in diameter brass curtain rings, sewing thread and black buttonhole thread. If you do not have any of the threads listed, you may wish to reduce the number of colours you buy or select from the ones you have.

Using the chart overleaf, trace the outline, curved vines and diamond-patterned markings onto the wrong side of the fabric with white dressmakers' tracing paper; trace one large curtain as shown and the other as the mirror image. Trace the narrow curtains up to the broken line shown on the chart only; make two of these. Tack (baste) over the traced lines so that the markings are visible on the right side of the fabric. Mount your fabric in a frame (see pages 158–159) and work the design following the instructions on page 17.

Stitch the grapevine border as shown in the diagram below and referring to the photograph, if necessary. Use dark green whipped backstitch for the main stem. Work the leaf stems with two backstitches, then bring the thread

Fig. 4   Grapevine Border Design

fold line

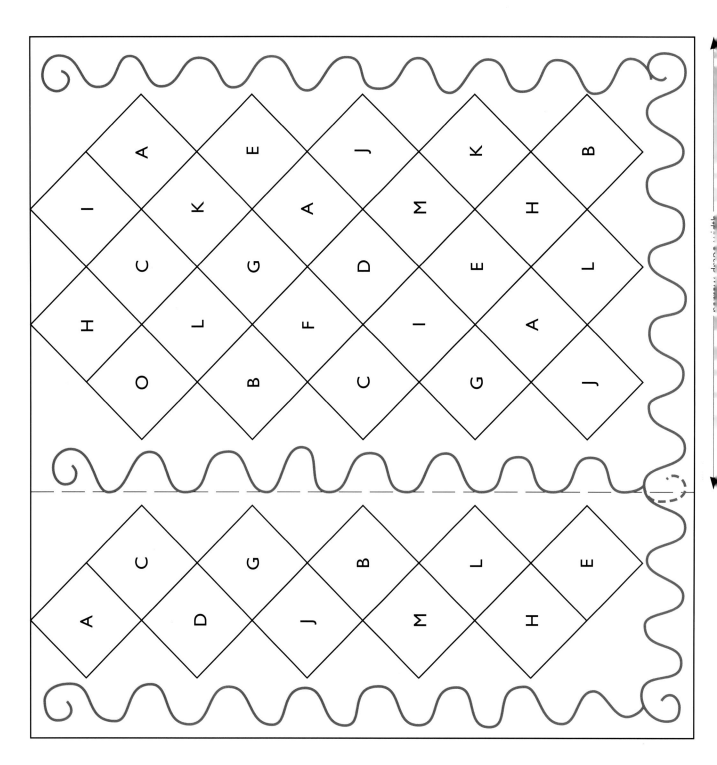

fold line

Fig. 5   Bedding Set
Marking Chart

Fig. 6 Embroidered Flowers
Embroider the flowers as explained here, referring to the placing indicated on the chart. (See page 158 for embroidery stitch instructions).

KEY DMC stranded cotton

White		Light clover green	369
Lemon yellow	307	Warm green	704
Hot yellow	742	Pale green	703
Orange	740	Spring green	702
Light orange	722	Dark green	700
Rose pink	223	Mid green	320
Pink	604	Mid sap green	907
Dark red	304	Dark sap green	905
Mid blue	798	Violet	3746
Light blue	799	Lilac	553
Very light green	472	Black	310
Clover green	367		

A Cowslip

A Work the stem and leaf veins of the cowslip in whipped backstitch in very light green and the flower bases as two straight stitches into the same holes in the same colour. Use pale green satin stitch for the leaves and for the flowers work three short stitches in a fan shape in hot yellow.

B Daffodil

B Work the leaves and flower stems of the daffodil in spring green whipped backstitch. For the outer flower petals work two straight stitches in the same holes in lemon yellow. Work the trumpet as four straight stitches, fanned out slightly at the outer end then add four single-turn French knots at the edges of the trumpet.

C Bluebell

C Work the leaves and flower stems in whipped backstitch using pale green. Work the flowers in light blue short straight stitches; start at the top with two stitches in the same holes, then work two stitches fanned very slightly at the open end (twice), then three stitches fanned out slightly (twice or three times). The flowers should become slightly larger and more spread out as you work down the stem.

D Carnation

D Work the stem and leaves of the carnation in whipped backstitch using mid green. Using the same green work the flower base as three straight stitches into the same hole by the stem but fanned slightly at the top. For the flower work five groups of three straight stitches, each group in the same hole at the base, using light orange.

E Thistle

E Work the stem of the thistle in mid green whipped backstitch and the leaves in feather stitch, starting at the outer end. At the flower base work a small double cross stitch in the same green. Work the flower heads in violet straight stitch.

F Clover

F Work the stems of the clover in mid green whipped backstitch. Work the leaves in clover green satin stitch. For the flowers make straight stitches in rose pink with two straight stitches in mid green at the base.

G Daisy

G Work the stems of the daisy in warm green whipped backstitch and work the leaves in satin stitch. For the flower centres work two-turn French knots in lemon yellow and work the flower petals in white straight stitch.

H Violet

H Work the stems and leaf stems of the violet in mid sap green whipped backstitch and the heart-shaped leaves in satin stitch using dark green. For the flower centres work two-turn French knots in lemon yellow and work the petals in lilac straight stitch.

I Marigold

I Work the stems and leaf stems of the marigold in whipped backstitch using mid sap green and the leaves in satin stitch using dark sap green. Work a lemon yellow double cross stitch for the flower centre and for the petals work straight stitches in orange round the yellow centre.

J Forget-me-not

J Work the stem of the forget-me-not in whipped backstitch using mid sap green and the leaves in satin stitch using dark green. Work a white single-turn French knot for each flower centre and add four petals around it with mid blue single-turn French knots.

K Rose

K Work the stem and leaf stems of the rose in whipped backstitch using mid sap green, and work the leaves in satin stitch using dark sap green. For the bud base work two straight stitches into the same hole at the base with mid sap green. Work a double cross stitch for the flower centre in lemon yellow and then work the five petals and flower bud in satin stitch using white or pink. Add the sepals as a straight stitch between each pair of petals in dark sap green. Add the thorns with short straight stitches in the same colour.

L Poppy

L Work the stem and leaf stems of the poppy in whipped backstitch using warm green then work three straight stitches for each leaf in spring green. For the bud base work two straight stitches into the same hole at the base in warm green. Work the flower centre as a double cross stitch in black and work four petals and the flower bud in dark red satin stitch.

M Strawberry

M Work the stems and leaf stems of the strawberry in whipped backstitch using warm green and work the leaves as three groups of five straight stitches, each group into the same hole at the base, using spring green. For the flower centre work a single-turn French knot in lemon yellow and add the four petals each with a single-turn French knot in white. For the strawberry use satin stitch in dark red with two straight stitches in spring green at the base for the sepals.

out just beyond the second backstitch and whip back through them in spring green. For the leaves work five straight stitches in a fan shape using warm green. Now turn to the grapes. Work bunches of 5-6 single-turn French knots, alternating a bunch of lilac with a bunch of light clover green and with two bunches on one side of the stem, then two on the other and so on.

Once all the embroidery is complete remove all the tacking threads and wash carefully then dry and press the embroideries between two pressing cloths or tea towels. Cut out the pieces, leaving a hem allowance of ½-¾in all round each one. Fold over the hem allowance and pin or press carefully. Next cut the lining material to match but leave a smaller hem allowance. Fold the

hem allowance over, and pin it to the back of each drape, making sure the lining and drape are flat. Make the lining slightly smaller all round than the embroidered drape so it will not show on the right side. Slipstitch the lining in place with sewing thread, making sure the stitches do not show on the right side. Use black buttonhole thread to stitch the curtain rings to the top edge of the drape at intervals of about ¾-1in. The drapes can be hung on wooden or brass rods.

MATCHING BED VALANCE

Make this valance to go round the top of the bed using materials left over from the drapes. The valance and lining are cut as one. First make a pattern by tracing the valances from the marking chart given with the bed hangings (page 16) onto folded paper, with the broken line on the fold. Add the grapevine pattern to one side only. Trace your pattern onto the wrong side of the fabric with a dressmakers' pen, allowing an extra ½in all round for seams – trace the outlines as well as the grapevine pattern. Tack the traced lines using sewing cotton so that the markings are visible on the right side of the fabric. Embroider two long valance pieces and one short piece in the same way as for the drapes.

Remove all the tacking threads and wash carefully. Dry and press the embroidery between two pressing cloths, then cut out the pieces, leaving ½in all round for seams. Fold each valance piece in half, right sides facing, and stitch the sides together, checking the length of the valance fits your bed and adjusting as necessary. Do not stitch the long edge. Turn each valance to the right side and press flat.

Cut a piece of black silk the size of your bed tester (the top of the bed) plus ½in on the sides and bottom edge where the valance pieces will fit, and add 1in to the other short end. Fold and press ½in under all round, including the top short end. Pin the valance pieces to the top, with the hem allowance on the underside. Tack the pieces in position. Cut lining to fit the top of the bed as well as the fold at the bed head and add a ¼in hem allowance all round. Fold the allowance under, and pin it to the back of the bed top, making sure the lining and bed top are flat, and enclosing the raw edges of the valance. Slipstitch the lining in place with black sewing thread, making sure you catch the valance pieces in position at the same time. Attach short lengths of

buttonhole thread to each side of the valance pieces and the fold at the bed head to tie the valances in position. Press the finished piece, then position it on the top of the bed. Tie the buttonhole thread in bows to hold the valances in position.

MATCHING BED COVER

This smart bed cover completes the floral bedding set. Cut out your main bed cover piece using the pattern given for the velvet bed cover (see page 13) and work a grapevine border and a grapevine centre medallion in the same way as for the bed drapes. Remove all tacking threads then wash, dry and press the embroidery between two pressing cloths or clean tea towels.

Machine stitching may make tiny pulls in your silk so assemble the bed cover by hand as follows. Cut out the bed cover, leaving a hem allowance of ½in all round. Cut lining fabric the same size, using your embroidered piece as a pattern. Fold over and press the hem allowances to the wrong side on each piece. Pin the lining in place on the wrong side, covering the turned hems of the embroidery and making sure the bed cover lies flat. Slipstitch the lining to the bed cover with sewing thread, making sure the stitches do not show on the right side. Press the finished piece carefully.

CUSHIONS

Cushions were plentiful during this period and were strewn about everywhere so make several for your room setting to be placed on furniture and stacked on the floor. Seat cushions were also used throughout this period, but only the more elaborate chairs of the most important members of the household might come complete with cushions. Although these were often made from fabric or hand worked design (see the chair in the Stuart drawing room, page 28) leather was also a popular covering.

FABRIC CUSHIONS

The cushion on top of the chest was made from a piece of cotton velvet taken from an old patchwork sampler while a patch of silk from the same sampler made the ideal backing. To make a similar cushion first measure the width and depth of your chest or other piece of furniture. Add an extra 1in to each dimension for seam allowances. Cut fabric and lining to the size you calculated and pin together with right sides facing. Hand sew the sides and ends using running stitch, taking a ½in seam allowance and leaving a gap to turn through. Turn out the cushion and fill with a suitable stuffing such as rice or salt. Close the gap with blind herringbone stitch or slip-stitch, then edge the cushion in gold with a single strand

of DMC cotton pearl. To attach the 'cord' lay it along the seam of the cushion and couch it in place with matching thread (see page 159).

Make the small red cushion on the chair in the same way from fabric and lining 3⅛ x 2¾in but omit the cord trim. The mauve cushion shown on the chest is 3½ x 1⅞in; the small red cushion on the chair is 2⅛ x 1¾in.

X LEATHER CHAIR CUSHION

To make this simple no-sew cushion you will need a scrap of new or preferably old soft leather, ⅛in thick balsa wood, cotton wool, thin foam or tissue paper and multi-purpose glue. Simply cut a block just under the dimensions of your chosen chair seat from ⅛in thick balsa wood. Our cushion block was 1½ x 1¼in. From a scrap of leather cut a piece ¼in larger all round (2 x 2¾in) – this allows enough for turnings. Trim the leather diagonally at the corners in the turning allowances. Place a small piece of cotton wool, thin foam or tissue on top of the balsa wood for padding, then wrap the cushion block with the leather, gluing each edge on the underside and making sure that the corners are stretched so that no raw edges show. Once in position the result will look most convincing.

X CARPET OVER THE AMBRY

The no-sew tapestry 'carpet' covering the ambry (storage chest) was made from a piece of modern upholstery fabric. To make one, simply measure the width and depth of the top of the chest and add extra for a short overhang at the sides, if desired. Cut the fabric to fit and fuse a lightweight backing fabric, such as fusible interfacing, onto the back to prevent fraying.

WALL HANGINGS

Although originally used for eliminating draughts, wall hangings became valued as works of art. Like furniture they were handed down from generation to generation but with the advent of more permanent home making during the reign of Queen Elizabeth I even greater demand was put upon the supply of quality tapestries. Many were still produced in England, with a leading tapestry weaving works well established in Warwick, but now many more were imported from major weaving centres such as Antwerp.

X PHOTOCOPIED WALL HANGING

If you are not inclined to hand work your own miniature tapestry the process of photocopying onto fabric can produce a most convincing result. To make this type of hanging all you need is a photograph of a tapestry and a piece of plain pure cotton fabric of A4 size. (The fabric must be exactly this size as this is the size of the photocopy bed.) Probably you will want your finished fabric hanging much smaller than A4 so it might be an idea to produce a number of tapestries, rugs or carpets at one time, arranging and gluing your original pictures onto an A4 piece of paper before going to the photocopy shop.

First either find a picture of a real tapestry or wall hanging in a magazine, catalogue or book or take a photograph of an original yourself. Beware at this stage of copyright laws which protect other people's work (you cannot sell a hanging you have made from a photograph of someone else's work). Next make either a colour photocopy on paper of the picture or produce a colour print of the photograph you have taken. In both cases enlargement or reduction of the picture can be made at this point to represent the actual size of the finished miniature. Take this, along with an A4 size piece of plain, all-cotton fabric, to a photocopy shop which prints pictures onto T-shirts or tea towels. Ask them to copy your picture onto your fabric. Then simply cut out your wall hanging which can either be glued to the front of a pole or fixed directly onto the wall. (As an added bonus the photocopying process protects the fabric from fraying.)

EMBROIDERED WALL HANGING

As an alternative to the photocopied hanging shown in our room set you might like to make an embroidered version. Note that bright colours, elaborate decoration and patterns of flowers and stylised plants were favoured in Tudor wall hangings. Gold was also used, often as threads or braid for scrolling patterns or as spangles (tiny sequins). This design, by Alison Larkin (see photograph, p22), is intended as a wall hanging, but could be used for a bed cover and drapes as well. It can be extended by adding another panel or made using two panels for a portière (door curtain). If your house is set at a time later than the Tudor period such a wall hanging could always be considered as an old family heirloom.

To make the hanging you will need a 12in square of green cotton or polyester-cotton fabric, a piece the same size of the same fabric or unbleached cotton lawn for lining, fine gold Jap-type thread, yellow or gold sewing cotton for couching, eight ¼in diameter brass rings, an embroidery hoop, transfer pencil and stranded cottons in the colours listed in the key. (The original was stitched in Anchor cottons; the DMC threads are equivalents.)

Use tracing paper or a transfer pencil to trace the black scrolling design from the chart in Fig. 7 onto your fabric. Using the sewing cotton, couch the gold Jap-type thread over the traced lines, taking the gold thread through to the back at the end of each scroll (see page 159). If the thread is quite thick you only need one, but if your thread is very fine lay two lengths side by side along the design lines. Do not let them cross over.

Position the leaves and flowers as shown in the chart and work them as explained in the key (see opposite). Remove the finished embroidery from the hoop and wash if necessary. Once dry, press gently on the reverse side between two pressing cloths or tea towels to prevent damage to the gold thread.

Trim the hanging to size, leaving about ½in at the bottom for a hem; turn under the hem and press gently.

Now trim the lining to match and turn under a hem, making the lining just smaller than the front piece. Stitch the lining fabric to the back of the hanging using slipstitch, and mitring the corners to keep them as flat as possible. Stitch the brass rings along the top of the hanging at regular intervals and press the hanging once more. Hang your finished piece in the room from a miniature curtain pole.

KEY   Stranded cotton

Colour	Anchor	DMC	Colour	Anchor	DMC
Green	229	701	Yellow	305	973
Red	022	815	White	white	blanc

Leaves Stitch in green, working four straight stitches into the same hole at one end with the other ends spread out to form a triangular shape.

Cherries Work in red with two-twist French knots.

Flowers: Work the centres in yellow with two-twist French knots and add the petals in white, working detached chain stitches around each flower centre. (See page 158 for embroidery stitch instructions).

Fig. 7   Cherry Vine Hanging Pattern

foldline for hanging edge

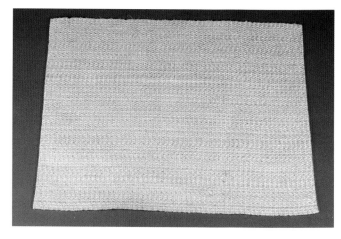 WOVEN RUSH MATTING

Woven and embroidered wool carpets were not widely produced in Europe until the seventeenth century so this Elizabethan bedroom has woven rush matting on the floor which was more typical of the time. You will need a loom and some weaving knowledge to make this woven mat.

Use sewing thread for the warp yarn which is placed on the loom. Cotton thread is best, but cotton-wrapped polyester works quite well. You can also use rayon sewing machine embroidery thread. You will need thread in five shades of pale greens and tans. The warp length is two yards and the width is 6⅛in. The set is 60 ends per inch and the reed is ideally 20 dpi at 3 per dent although 15 dpi at 4 per dent is also acceptable (reed marks are more noticeable, but not objectionable due to the plaited look of the rush). The number of ends is 370. Use the same type of sewing thread for the weft in medium beige or medium olive depending on how old the rush is supposed to look.

To weave the mat, designed by Bonni Backe, first wind the warp with all 5 colours, keeping the spools in separate jars on the floor to prevent tangling. If they still jump out, then you will need 5 plastic lidded containers (such as margarine tubs). Make a nice round hole in the lid, pass the thread through and snap the lid on. As you form the cross, keep the 1 x 1 cross, but vary the order of the colours at each pass. Weave the rush matting about ½in longer than the desired finished length, off tension. For ½in at the beginning and end of the rug weave a heading of 2/2 basket weave. After weaving, cut off, leaving extra warp outside the heading, and steam press the rug. Apply Aleene's Liquid Fusible Web to the wrong side of the heading, following the instructions on the bottle. Once dry, trim the heading to ¼in then press the hem back even with the beginning of the twill weave.

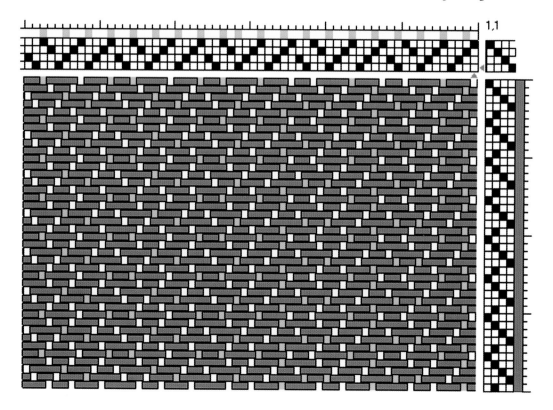

Fig. 8   Woven Rush Matting

TUDOR FEAST

Set at around 1590, this room might belong to a yeoman farmer and form part of a more modest home than the previous one. The walls are of crude plasterwork and the floor is made of brick or stone but there is a tapestry hanging on the wall and other evidence of soft furnishings which proves that this is not the poorest home. In addition there is a cloth covering the top of the boarded press and another on the table while a soft velvet cushion adds comfort to the stool at the table end, a luxury enjoyed only by the head of the household. In the scene a special feast or celebration banquet is about to take place. Pewter cups and dishes, together with an array of lavish foods, shows that this is a comfortably well-off family although not extremely wealthy. (The pigs would not actually inhabit a room such as this but have wandered into forbidden territory from another area.)

The room is of a simple construction, being just three walls, floor and ceiling which could be a room in any suitable dolls' house. To create the large, deep open fire-

This simple room is furnished with a few Tudor style items mostly made by '9'. The pewter tableware is by Tony Knott and the delicious foods are from Rosie Duck Designs (see page 165 for details).

place a short false wall was added, protruding from the side and then linked to the back wall by another section across the top. The walls have all been roughened by smearing crack filler over them and then finished with a light sanding and coat of flat emulsion paint. Dark stained strips or randomly carved wood have been attached where joists and beams should be and the stone floor was cut from pre-finished resin sheeting. For this room set we made the table and cupboard covers, the bench cushion and tapestry hanging.

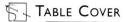 TABLE COVER

To see a cloth on the 'boards' in such a humble room one might imagine that a very important guest must be expected to share the feast. Hopefully roast suckling pig is not on the menu! To make this table cover you will need some finely woven cotton, matching thread, domestic plastic film and spray starch.

Cut a piece of finely woven cotton to the size of the table plus about 2½in all round for the drop. Turn a hem by rolling each edge of the fabric between your fingers and sew in place with blind herringbone stitch. Press the cover and steam the hem; do not press the hem flat. To shape the cover first protect the 'boards' with a piece of domestic plastic film, then place the cover on top and spray with starch to fashion the side drop.

X CARPET OVER THE CUPBOARD

A 'tapestry' carpet covering the cupboard adds a touch of colour and can be made from a piece of modern upholstery fabric. You do not need any sewing skills. Simply cut your fabric to the desired length to cover the top and drop over the ends by approximately 1in. We frayed the ends of the cover for an attractive finish. To do this just pull out the cross threads with a pin until the fringe is the desired length. Fuse backing fabric, such as lightweight fusible interfacing or fine cotton, onto the back of the fabric to prevent further fraying, if desired. If you are using cotton backing you will need to apply fusible bonding fabric such as Bondaweb, following the manufacturer's instructions.

BENCH CUSHION

Pieces of cotton velvet were taken from an old patchwork sampler to make the top and back of the cushion shown on the stool at the end of the table. The head of the household or important visitor would sit in comfort here. To make the cushion you will need old pieces of cotton velvet, a suitable stuffing such as rice or salt, matching thread, gold sewing thread and DMC pearl cotton in gold for a trim.

Measure the area on the piece of furniture to be cushioned and cut two pieces of fabric to size, adding a ¼in seam allowance all round. Our finished cushion was 2⅛ x 1¾in so we started with two 2⅝ x 2¼in rectangles of fabric. Pin the right sides of the two pieces together and hand sew the sides and ends in running stitch, leaving a gap for turning. Turn and fill the cushion with stuffing such as rice or salt. Close the gap with blind herringbone stitch. Edge the cushion in gold with a single strand of DMC pearl cotton. To attach the 'cord' to the cushion lay it along the seam and use matching thread to couch it in place.

X TAPESTRY HANGING

Although probably too grand for this fairly modest room, we might imagine that the tapestry has been hung in honour of an important occasion or visitor. It appears a most convincing miniature but is in fact a photocopy on fabric which you can easily make yourself. The project requires no sewing skills. For instructions on making a photocopied hanging see the Elizabethan Bedroom, page 21.

STUART DRAWING ROOM

The date of this drawing room is actually carved on the back of the jointed armchair: 1649. The walls are panelled and stained a dark colour while the ceiling has moulded plasterwork and the floor is polished boarding. Light streams into the room through the window which is fairly large and which has rectangular glass panes, each set in a frame of lead. An upholstered Farthingale chair stands by the window and a woven carpet adorns the floor. The owner is reasonably well-to-do as can be seen from the exquisitely dressed figure.

To construct this room sections of pre-cast plaster-moulded panels were used which were linked together

A selection of solid oak furniture by David Hurley lines the dark panelled walls in this Stuart drawing room. Traditionally these might be moved into the centre if required. The figure is by Jill Bennett (see page 165 for contact details).

and stained and polished to represent wood. The floor was cut from a readily available sheet of wooden flooring strips and again finished with a polish. Miniature wooden mouldings were used for the ceiling and to create the window structure. Strips of lead were cut and stuck to clear plastic to form the lead framed panes of glass and off white flat emulsion paint was applied to the ceiling to give a plastered finish.

The soft furnishings in this room comprise the luxurious but easy to make velvet curtain, fabric carpet, chair cushion and crewel work floor cushion plus an upholstered Farthingale chair.

VELVET CURTAIN

By 1600 in larger houses floor-length curtains were generally used, often made from plain or patterned velvets. In this drawing room a curtain of deep red cotton velvet has been chosen. As this curtain is hung within the miniature and not on a front opening section it will not be in for close scrutiny, so the simplest but most effective way for creating it has been used which does not require any sewing. To make it you will need cotton velvet, a Pretty Pleater, spray starch, fusible bonding fabric such as Bondaweb, multi-purpose glue, a curtain pole and glass-headed pins.

Take a measurement from the top of the curtain pole to the floor (in this case 8in) and measure the width of the whole window (6in). Add an extra 1in to the length to allow for ½in turnings both top and bottom. Cut two curtains this size (9 x 6in). Stitch or fuse the ½in hems at top and bottom in place. (For details on fusing hems see the instructions for the curtains in the Regency dining room, page 56.) Making sure the velvet pile runs from top to bottom, use a Pretty Pleater to form the curtain pleats (see page 161). Your first side pleat should be a little over width, standing up from the pleater so that it can be used to form a side hem. If the pleats are slightly irregular this is all to the good as it adds that touch of realism. When the pleating is completed spray with starch and either press with an iron or leave to dry naturally. Once dry remove the curtain from the pleater and glue the top to the curtain pole within the room, extending or condensing the pleats concertina style into the desired position before the glue is dry. Glass-headed pins can be used to hold the curtain at this stage and removed later. Glue the side hems in place to finish.

CHAIR CUSHION

By 1649 the notion of completely or partly upholstered chairs had been established. The chair against the back wall of the room has a separate cushion on the seat in a brocade fabric which was made in the same way as the leather chair cushion in the Elizabethan bedroom (page 21) except that it had to be adjusted to fit round the arm supports. To do this cut small notches out of the cushion block and shape the fabric to fit. Fabric will not stretch in the same way as leather so you need to form corner folds within the notches at the back of the cushion. If done neatly the cushion should just slide into position with no need for gluing.

FABRIC CARPET

In larger houses between 1600 and 1660 most floors were of polished timber, often covered by a rug or carpet. These were still expensive but increasingly many were imported from Turkey or Persia. The one in this room has been created simply by cutting a patterned section from a larger piece of printed upholstery fabric. To prevent the edges from fraying we applied liquid Fray Check to the outer edge of the selected pattern and allowed it to dry before cutting out. Alternatively you can fuse backing fabric to the back of the carpet which does the same job. Either use lightweight iron-on interfacing for this purpose or use cotton fabric, fusing it in place with fusible webbing (Bondaweb), following the manufacturer's instructions.

FARTHINGALE CHAIR

Chairs of this style were most popular around the mid-seventeenth century. The miniature example in this room was made by Escutcheon but for extra detail it can be re-upholstered. All you need is paper, fabric, narrow ribbon, Fray Check and fabric glue.

First make a paper pattern of the existing leather covers by placing small pieces of paper onto the back and seat of the chair and tracing through. Remember to include all the area covered by the leather. Trim the paper patterns to the exact size of the leather pieces and then pin them to your chosen fabric, making sure that any pattern is nicely centred. Cut out the fabric. Glue the fabric only around the edges, positioning it over the existing leather and making sure no glue gets onto the centre of the fabric.

To make matching fringing cut a strip of fabric about ½in wide which is long enough to trim both the seat and back and carefully fray it along one edge until a suitable fringe has been made. Apply liquid Fray Check to prevent further fraying. Carefully cut and glue this fringing around the seat and the back of the chair and then cover the top raw edge by gluing on a finishing piece of narrow ribbon. Bought fringing can also be used to trim the chair but do be sure it is small enough and in scale.

ORCHARD FLOOR CUSHION

If you have basic embroidery and sewing skills you can make this splendid floor cushion designed by Alison Larkin which is sure to brighten up your room set. Alternatively, make one from decorative upholstery fabric and omit the embroidery. To make the cushion you will need dark green fine cotton fabric, matching thread, ecru stranded embroidery cotton for the edging cord, DMC stranded embroidery cottons in the colours given in the key, Fray Check and suitable filling such as toy stuffing.

Cut a 4½in square of fabric and find the centre by folding it in half in each direction. Trace the pattern from the marking chart onto the fabric using dressmakers'

Fig. 9   Orchard Floor Cushion Chart and Key

Silver interlaced chain stitch, laced both sides

Silver interlaced chain stitch, laced on outer side only

Silver whipped backstitch

Deep mauve (208) single-turn French knot

White single-turn French knot

Pink (350) straight stitch

Mid red (352) straight stitch

Mid green (702) straight stitch

Yellow (727), single-turn French knot

Deep red (815) single-turn French knot

Dark brown (829) whipped backstitch

Light brown (841) whipped backstitch

Light green (993) whipped backstitch (strawberry stems) or straight stitch (mulberry leaves)

Dark green (3345) straight stitch

Strawberry Work the stems using whipped backstitch in light green then add the leaves with straight stitches worked into the same holes using mid green. Work the flowers using single-turn French knots in yellow and white. For the strawberries work five straight stitches into one hole in mid red and add two straight stitches in light green for the sepals.

Peach Work the trunk and branches with four lines of whipped backstitch in light brown. Add leaves with three straight stitches in dark green. For the peaches work five straight stitches in peach and pink (three in one colour and two in the other but vary the order), shaped to make a circle.

Mulberry Work the trunk with four lines of whipped backstitch in light brown. Add leaves with one straight stitch then six angled short stitches in light green. For the fruits work bunches of single-turn French knots in deep red.

Apple Work the trunk and leaves like the peach tree and work the apples in the same way as the peaches but use mid green and mid red.

Grape Work the trunk and branches in whipped backstitch using dark brown then work the leaves as five straight stitches worked into the same hole using mid-green. For the grapes work eight single-turn French knots in dark mauve.

Peach   Mulberry

Grape   Apple

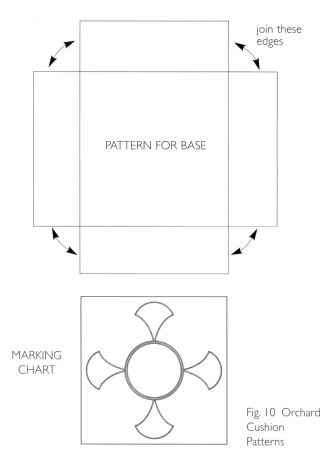

join these edges

PATTERN FOR BASE

MARKING CHART

Fig. 10 Orchard Cushion Patterns

tracing paper or a fine quilters' marker pen. Mount it in a card frame or hoop (see page 156). Using one strand of the silver stranded thread stitch the centre circle in interlaced chain stitch, laced on both sides. Stitch the outer arcs in interlaced chain laced on the outer edge only and the joining arcs in whipped backstitch (see page 158). Using one strand of embroidery cotton, stitch the rest of the design as given in Fig. 9.

Trim the embroidery to about ⅛in from the stitching to allow for a seam. Now cut out the base fabric using the pattern above, adding ⅛in seam allowances all round, and seal the edges with Fray Check. Sew up the short

edges with right sides together to shape the base, taking a ½in seam allowance. Sew the cushion top in position on three sides. Now turn the cushion the right way out and fill with your choice of filler – toy stuffing or cotton wool. Slipstitch the last side closed.

Make a twisted cord from about 20in of stranded cotton using four strands of dark green and four strands of ecru. To do this, knot four strands of each colour together at each end. Pin one end of both sets to a firm base, such as a pinboard, and put a pencil or knitting needle through the other end. Pulling the cord fairly firmly, use the pencil to twist the cord and keep twisting until the cord buckles in the middle. Hold the middle of the cord and bring the two ends together. The cord should twist all by itself when you let go of the middle. If it is not tight enough separate the ends again and twist a bit more.

Stitch the cord over the join between the base and cushion top using dark green sewing cotton. Leave a loop of about ¼in long at the corners, stitching firmly over both sides of the loop. Stitch several time over the ends of the cord when you have taken it right round the cushion to hold the ends, then trim the cord ends. Finally, cut through the loops at the corners and tease out the thread to make the tassels.

 DAISY BLACKWORK FLOOR CUSHION

As an alternative to the floor cushion in our room set you might like to try making this striking version designed by Alison Larkin (shown right) which is a bit easier to stitch. It only requires two colours of embroidery cotton (floss), making it a good choice if you do not have any suitable cottons in your work box. You will need some Salamanca (50-count) ivory evenweave linen, black machine embroidery thread, black stranded cotton, (DMC 310), gold stranded embroidery cotton, such as Madeira 5012, crimson cotton fabric for the backing, red sewing cotton, a little toy stuffing or cotton wool, Fray Check and a size 26 tapestry needle and fine sewing needle. You can make a larger cushion if you like using 36-count fabric.

Mount your fabric in a frame, if desired, (see page 156) then work the blackwork design as shown in the chart, using machine embroidery thread and the tapestry needle. Each square on the chart represents one stitch worked over two threads of linen, giving a final stitch count of 25 stitches per inch. Stitch the outlines first using whipped backstitch, then complete the infills using straight stitch. Finally, stitch the flowers using backstitch for the stems and leaf outlines and lazy daisy stitch for the petals (see page 158 for details on working embroidery stitches). With one strand of gold thread and the tapestry needle, stitch the gold details, using a single-turn French knot for the flower centres and backstitch for the leaf veins.

Cut out the backing fabric using the patterns given below right, adding ½in seam allowance all round. Seal the cut edges with Fray Check. Stitch the short edges together with right sides facing, taking a ½in seam allowance. This shapes the base. Trim the cushion

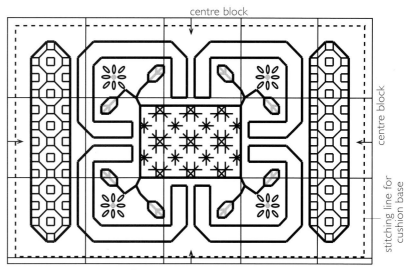

Fig. 11   Blackwork Floor Cushion Design
KEY   Stranded cotton and machine embroidery thread
—   Black (whipped backstitch)   Lazy daisy and French knot
—   Black (straight stitch)   Gold backstitch

top to ½in from the stitching line, then stitch the cushion top to the base on three sides. Turn the cushion right side out and stuff gently with toy stuffing. Do not over fill. Slipstitch the last side closed.

Make a twisted cord using three strands of black stranded cotton and three strands of gold thread, following the instructions for the cord trim on the Orchard Floor Cushion (see page 30). Stitch the cord over the join between the base and cushion top using machine embroidery thread. Leave a loop of cord about ¼in long at the corners and stitch firmly over both sides of the loop. Stitch several time over the ends of the cord when you have taken it right round the cushion to hold the ends, then trim the ends. Finally, cut through the loops at the corners and tease out the thread to make the tassels.

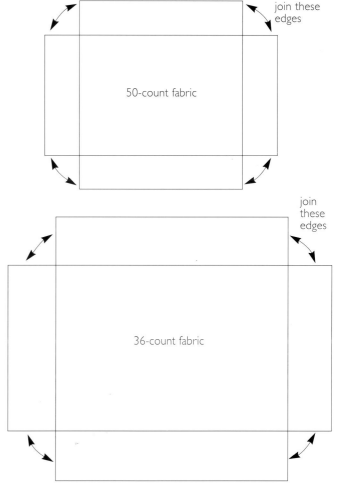

Fig. 12   Blackwork Cushion Base Pattern

31

GEORGIAN STYLE

THE PERIOD 1714–1810 covers the reigns of George I to George IV when the wealthy were able to travel for pleasure and bring back ideas and objects for the home from abroad. Money was available for decorating to the highest standards of elegance and architects and designers could be hired to build and decorate the home down to the last detail. Trade in textiles flourished and the use of fabrics in the home increased many fold in the form of tablecloths, linen bedding and drapery linings, paired curtains with pelmets and valences, pull-up blinds, wall coverings and carpets. Ever increasing sophistication in production techniques led to an even greater choice of textiles. Matching or complementary fabrics were often used to co-ordinate bed hangings, wall coverings, curtains and pelmets and for upholstery. Available fabrics included lightweight silks, cotton chintzes, linen cloth, lace, damasks, velvets and brocades. Often these would be embroidered or embellished with gold or silver threads or elegant appliquéd designs.

❋　　❋　　❋

After a brief period of English Baroque style as seen in the work of Vanbrugh and Hawksmoor it was perhaps Palladian architecture which gained the greatest popularity during the first part of the eighteenth century. First brought to England in the seventeenth century by Inigo Jones, a number of eighteenth-century architects adapted the classical Roman style of sixteenth-century Italian architect Andrea Palladio. Built large or small in town or country Palladian style appeared everywhere. Its classical Roman proportions and symmetry together with its sometimes ornate detailing made houses appear solid and established. Rooms were furnished with sometimes large and heavy pieces of furniture which included bookcases and the still important bedstead, all embellished with

popular architectural features. Smaller pieces such as chairs and settees were now upholstered in velvet, damask, or most often in needlework depicting floral landscape or portrait designs. From 1727 to 1740 the work of William Kent dominated the furniture scene but from 1740 until about 1760 the name of Thomas Chippendale became synonymous with good furniture design.

As the century advanced, those able to travelled still further and increased their knowledge of the ancient world. It became apparent that it was Greece, not Rome, that held the origins of classical forms and that this style was even purer. As a result Greek together with Roman style influences were popular and either existed side by side or blended into original forms. Perhaps best known

This Georgian drawing room is decorated in Palladian style which was much admired at the time. The furniture, from David Booth, is in the style of Thomas Chippendale. Architectural details were supplied by Sue Cook and the figures were made and dressed by Jill Bennett (see page 165).

for his work and influence during the later Georgian period was James Wyatt, who completed designs in all manner of styles which included that based on Greek classicism, and Robert Adam who dominated the architectural field from 1760 to 1790. It was Adam who really started the concept of interior design, using the themes and influences of the day but also working carpet and ceiling designs together or creating unusual shaped rooms of oval or circular forms. His ornamental or decorative work was often simple and featured patterned ceiling panels in a mixture of pastel colours. In the manner of a true interior designer Adam usually designed every aspect of a room from the walls, ceiling and floor finish to the furniture and furnishings.

GEORGIAN DRAWING ROOM

This is the drawing room of a wealthy middle-class house of around 1740-1750. The walls represent pine wood panels painted green and the ceiling is of stucco plaster. There are a number of architectural details in classical style in the form of the pediment above the door, the ceiling cornice, carved wall mouldings in the shape of panels, marble niches containing classically styled busts, fireplace and overmantle mirror. The window is a twelve-panelled sash draped with a pair of velvet curtains held back by gold cords. The mahogany chairs and settee are in the style of Chippendale and are upholstered in an antique silk fabric representing needlework. The tapestry carpet is a mid eighteenth century French Rococo design in keeping with the times, and the pole screen is also finished with a tapestry. The remaining items of furniture in the room together with the silver pieces would also date from the middle of the eighteenth century.

Lighting was by means of candle and in this room takes the form of a chandelier in the centre of the ceiling and decorative silver sconces by Terence Stringer, located on each side of the fireplace mirror. An accurate period look for this room has largely been achieved through the use of architectural details. The skirting board, chair rails and wall panels were formed from readily available miniature wood mouldings and the floor has been cut from a sheet of wood strip flooring.

Soft furnishings in the room comprise the pair of velvet curtains with gold ties and tassels, the covered seats of the chairs and sofa, the tapestry carpet and pole screen.

GEORGIAN-STYLE CURTAINS

Curtains in the middle of the eighteenth century were simply paired but looped and held back with one or more cords trimmed with tassels. They would be made of damask or a variety of velvets.

The simple, no-sew curtains in this room have been made in exactly the same manner as those in the Stuart drawing room (see page 28) except that as the curtain pole for the window measured 5½in, each curtain is 5½in wide and 7½in long. Simple cord tiebacks were made by gluing a length of braid at an appropriate height around each curtain and easing the curtain into shape using glass-headed pins to hold it temporarily. The tiny tassels on the tiebacks were made by forming loops of stranded cotton around a cocktail stick and tying them off securely at the top. The loops should be cut open at the bottom to the desired length. (For further curtain ideas see the Regency curtains on page 56.)

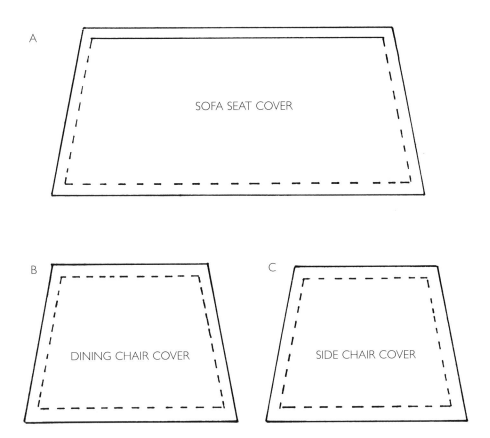

Fig. 13 Sofa and Chair Seat Patterns

 SOFA AND CHAIR SEATS

The seats of the Chippendale chair set we used from David Booth normally come beautifully finished but it might be an idea to re-upholster them in your own co-ordinating fabric. This is simple to do, requiring no sewing, but you need to work carefully because obviously the furniture is fragile.

Cut new covers from the patterns given above, centring any fabric pattern neatly. Lay out each fabric piece, wrong side up, and centre the corresponding seat pad face down on top. Fold the excess fabric over the pad around the edges and glue in place, paying special attention to corners to ensure a neat finish and trimming off the excess fabric here as necessary. Carefully replace the seat pads.

⋈ GEORGIAN-STYLE CARPET

This tapestry carpet design by Sue Bakker is based on an English pile carpet of the mid eighteenth century. Although carpets (both needle made and woven) with naturalistic floral designs continued to be made as late as the 1780s, the major revival of knotted pile carpets during the 1750s took designs from fashionable French Rococo designs. The Savonnerie carpet factory in Paris had been set up during the sixteenth century to weave carpets for the Louvre and to stem the flow of expensive Turkish and Persian carpets coming into France. Later, during the eighteenth century, the factory wove the great carpets for Louis XIV's new palace at Versailles. It was these designs which set the new fashionable style for the rest of the eighteenth century. By the mid eighteenth century a number of designers defected from the Savonnerie and set up or took over factories in Britain.

The design for this carpet is based on that type of French Rococo carpet. The central medallion is composed of leaves surrounded by a circle with more leaves draped over the edge of the ring. Elongated foliage fills the corners of the main field. This is quite a popular design but you could work the pattern given for the drawing room if you prefer (see page 42).

To make the carpet you will need canvas or gauze, a size 24 tapestry needle if you are using 22-count canvas and size 26 for 30 or 40-count silk gauze, an embroidery frame and DMC stranded cottons in the colours given in the key. Note: if you are using 22-count canvas the finished carpet will be 12¾ x 10in; on 30-count gauze it will be 9¼ x 7¼in and on 40-count gauze it will be 7 x 5½in.

One quarter of the finished design is shown in the chart. Simply continue the design for the other three quarters. It is easiest if you work the same motif in each quarter of the carpet one after the other, starting in the centre. Having worked the one from the chart, work the opposite one, then work the mirror motif and the last one the same. By that time you will have remembered the stitch progression.

One square of the chart equals one tent or half cross stitch. Bind the edges of the canvas to prevent the threads catching on them and mark the centre with tacking (basting) threads then mount your work in a

Fig. 14 Georgian-style Carpet Design
KEY DMC stranded cotton

	Symbol	Name	Number		Symbol	Name	Number
+	Mid pink	223		V	Palest gold	677
−	Pale pink	224			Mid gold	729
	Dark gold	420		•	Off white	822
/	Pale gold	676			Brown	839

	Symbol	Name	Number
O	Beige	842
X	Darkest gold	869
	Dark green	3362
	Mid green	3363

	Symbol	Name	Number
	Light green	3364
	Rose red	3721 + 3722

frame to keep it taut (see page 156). Following the chart, begin in the centre and work outwards. For more advice refer to Using a Chart, page 157. First work the detail in half cross stitch and then work the background in basketweave stitch. Start working with a 'waste' knot and end by threading the needle through the backs of previous stitches. The chart is designed so that you can usually work the outline to a motif and perhaps the central vein of a leaf and then fill in the rest. One of the leaves in the border has been left without the background green symbols so that the outline and leaf veins can be seen clearly.

To finish, first press or block the tapestry if necessary (see page 161). Trim the unworked canvas edges to ½in from the design and fold under the stitching. Oversew the edge of the canvas all the way around using four strands of the background colour. As you approach the corner of the canvas fold the adjacent edge under and sew through both thicknesses of the canvas. If you wish you can back the tapestry with lining, turning under a small fabric allowance around each edge and slipstitching it in place (see page 162).

EARLY GEORGIAN POLE SCREEN

Fireplaces were changing during this period (see the Regency Pole Screen, page 54) and so was its furniture and accessories. This fire screen is a relatively modern piece for the time, but its traditional tapestry design reflects the fact that it would have been made by hand, whereas the forward looking carpet would have been made in a factory. This original pattern by Sue Bakker is a typical floral design of the late seventeenth and early eighteenth centuries in England when flowers were intensely popular. The design shows an exotic plant with realistic and fantastic flowers and wind-swept leaves growing out of hummocks. The background here is off-white, but a very dark navy blue (DMC 939) or brown (DMC 3371) could also be used. On 48-count silk gauze the design is approximately 1⅝ x 1½in.

To copy this pole screen you will need a suitable screen, 48-count silk gauze, a No 10 embroidery (crewel) needle, DMC stranded embroidery cottons in the colours listed in the key, thin card, glue stick and an embroidery hoop or frame.

Either fix the gauze to a heavy cardboard frame (see page 156) or sew it to a piece of cotton and then put the whole thing in an embroidery hoop. Use one strand of embroidery cotton throughout and work the main design of the piece in half cross stitch and the background in basketweave stitch. Following the chart opposite, begin in the centre and work outwards. For more advice, refer to Using a Chart, page 157. Start working with a 'waste' knot and end by threading the needle through the backs of previous stitches.

To finish, cut a piece of thin card to fit into the well of the pole screen – you may find it helpful to trace the shape onto paper first to make a pattern. Cut round the outside of the stitching closely and carefully, leaving enough to wrap to the back of the card. Place the embroidery over the card, being careful to ensure that it is centred and exactly vertical and wrap the excess gauze to the back. Check the fit in the pole screen and trim the card if necessary, then carefully glue the fabric edges to the back of the card with glue stick. Place the mounted embroidery in position, easing the work under the lip of the recess with the blunt end of a needle.

Fig. 15 Early Georgian Pole Screen Design
KEY DMC stranded cotton

Mid pink	223	Brown	840	Light blue	932	Coral pink	3712
Light pink	224	Mid blue-green	926	Light green	3013	Dark blue-green	3768
Light gold	676	Light blue-green	927	Dark green	3051	Dark gold	3828
Mid gold	729	Mid blue	931	Mid green	3052	Background: 3033 (off-white) or 939 (navy) or 3371 (brown)

GEORGIAN MUSIC ROOM

Although coffee houses were growing in popularity, with card playing and gambling at its height, for most members of the wealthy classes in the eighteenth century the majority of entertainment was made at home. Embroidery, needlework, letter writing and taking tea were popular pastimes for ladies but the playing of musical instruments like the harpsichord or violin was something which could be enjoyed by all. This room has been created in late Georgian style for a fairly well-to-do household as a music room. It has plain pastel walls, an ornate fireplace and overmantle mirror, door surround with pediment, chair rail, frieze and ceiling cornice all embellished with gilded decoration, a stucco work ceiling and wood block floor. As in the drawing room the fireplace has an over-mantel mirror.

We chose to furnish the room with a perfectly styled breakfront bureau (not shown in the picture), tea table, side chairs, harpsichord and bench which were part of a Goebel Miniatures' Chippendale room set that is now no longer available. Produced in 1979 under the name of 'The Butterfly Collection' these pieces are actually made from plastic and are now sought after collector's items.

Soft furnishings made for the room comprise a curtain with ruched pelmet, embroidered pole screen, tapestry carpet and chair seat cover.

This music room would date from around 1785 and contains pieces of furniture from 'The Butterfly Collection' which are now collector's items. The music stand and Chippendale style chair with tapestry seat are all made by David Booth and the chandelier is by Phyllis Tucker (see page 166).

CORINTHIAN CARPET

Carpets or rugs, either hand worked with a needle or woven by machine, would definitely have graced a room such as this. Here the design by Lynne Parkinson reflects the popularity of Greek styles at the time. However, if you prefer you could make the carpet from our drawing room instead (see page 36). To make this carpet you will need an 11 x 8in rectangle of 22-count canvas, a No. 24 tapestry needle, sewing thread, masking tape, a small frame and DMC stranded embroidery cottons in the colours given in the key – you will need five skeins of the background colour, 932, 2 skeins of 3829 and 677, and one skein of 729 and 676.

Bind the edges of the canvas with masking tape to prevent the threads catching on the edges of the canvas and mark the centre with tacking (basting) threads. Mount the fabric in a frame (see page 156). Work the design from the centre (marked with a star) outwards, following the chart opposite and using three strands of cotton. Work in half cross stitch. Start with a 'waste' knot and end by threading the needle through the backs of previous stitches. For more advice, refer to Using a Chart, page 157. One square on the chart represents one stitch on the canvas. The chart shows half the design. Work this half then turn the chart around to work the other half.

To finish, first press or block the tapestry if necessary (see page 161). Trim the unworked canvas edges to ⅛in from the design and fold under the stitching. Oversew the edge of the canvas all the way around using four strands of the background colour. As you approach the corner of the canvas fold the adjacent edge under and sew through both thicknesses of the canvas. If you wish you can back the tapestry with a lining, turning under a small fabric allowance around each edge and slipstitching it in place (see page 162).

CURTAIN WITH RUCHED PELMET

By 1785 pull-up blinds or a form of ruched fabric pelmet above paired, straight curtains was a popular window dressing. We chose to use a pair of curtains topped with an

Fig. 16 Corinthian Carpet Design

KEY   DMC Stranded cotton

![Dark gold] Dark gold   3829   ☐ Mid gold   729   ▬ Light gold   676   • Very light gold   677   Blue background   932

interpretation of this latter type of pelmet, using a patterned silk. To make this window dressing you will need furnishing fabric, fusible bonding fabric (Bondaweb), a Pretty Pleater, spray starch, glue, pins and a curtain pole.

First measure the window and make the curtains in the same way as the velvet curtains in the Stuart drawing room (see page 28). Hang them on the curtain pole at the window. To make the pelmet cut a strip of fabric 2½in deep by the width of the window plus the depth of the moulding on both sides plus ½in. Pleat the fabric in the Pretty Pleater (see page 161) and then remove it and arrange the folds roughly. Glue under ¼in on each end and then glue one long edge to the top and sides of the window moulding. Using more glue, push the pleated fabric upwards in the middle to shape it, temporarily pinning it in place until the glue dries.

SIDE CHAIRS AND PIANO BENCH

As both the chairs and piano bench in this room are old collector's items it would be unwise to recover them. However, if you have contemporary miniatures you can remove the seat pads and re-upholster them in the same way as the chairs in the Georgian drawing room (see page 35). You do not need any sewing skills for this. Work carefully and do take time to centre the pattern of your fabric on the seat carefully.

POLE SCREEN

Pole screens were used to curb direct heat from the fire and most elegantly designed rooms would have one. In the eighteenth century these were usually embellished with embroidered pictures or floral designs. The pole screen in this room set is an inexpensive imported version with a fresh piece of tapestry fabric glued into its panel. To make a good base for a new piece of fabric simply trace the size of the frame opening onto paper to make a pattern and then cut the pattern from thin card. Do this carefully to ensure a neat fit.

Either work a tapestry design to fit the screen or select a suitable fabric. Cut your fabric or hand worked tapestry just larger than the card. Centre the fabric over the card and wrap the extra over to the back. Now check the fit in the pole screen and trim the card if necessary. Glue the fabric to the back of the card – glue stick is ideal for this. Finally, glue the covered card into the frame of the pole screen.

TAPESTRY CHAIR SEAT COVER

Pastoral scenes were a popular subject for embroidery and tapestry work during this period, so this pattern for a seat cover by Annelle Fergusson is ideal for a Georgian room setting. You can make this design for any room, even a bedroom, and because it uses a range of colours it should fit in with most colour schemes. However, you can always change the background colour of the border to suit your room scheme, if desired. To make it you will need 48-count silk gauze, a size 10 crewel needle, thin foam, multi-purpose glue and DMC embroidery cotton in the colours listed in the key.

This is a small project so it is easiest to sew it in a card frame (see page 156) rather than an embroidery hoop. Cut a card frame with a 2½in square opening and tape the gauze to it. Then very lightly outline the seat piece on the gauze. Using the chart opposite, work the design from the centre outwards. Work the pattern in tent stitch and

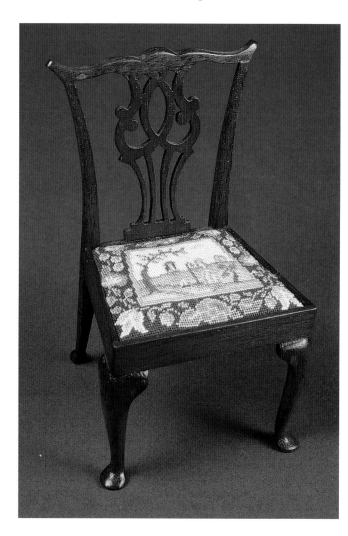

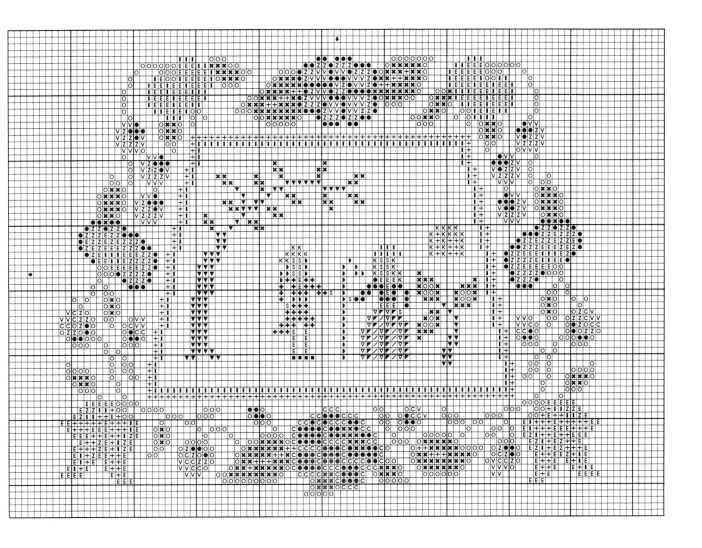

the background in basketweave stitch (see page 158) using one strand of cotton. Work the sky in sky blue (3759) and the landscape in greens (3051, 3052 and 3053), using the photograph as a guide. Work the background border in deep blue (3750). Take the background ¼in outside the outline of your chair seat but note that the corners may be mitred so you will produce a smoother finish if you omit the stitching in the corners of this extra area. (See also Using a Chart, page 157.)

Remove the finished piece from the card frame and steam press it. Leave to dry completely. Cut around the edge of the worked area leaving a ¼in border of unworked gauze. Cut thin foam to the size of the seat piece and lightly glue it to the seat piece. Centre the tapestry over the foam, fold the edges over gently and glue on all sides. Leave to dry. Finally, cut backing fabric to size and glue it to the back to protect the work and provide a neat finish.

Fig. 17 Tapestry Chair Seat Cover Design
KEY   DMC Stranded cotton

S	Dark flesh	407	O	Light green	3053
K	Brown	420	/	Very light blue	3753
+	Light gold	676	V	Cream	3770
✚	Dark gold	680	Z	Terracotta	3778
I	Mid gold	729	C	Light terracotta	3779
◗	Very dark brown	838	●	Medium peach	3830
■	Dark grey-green	844	E	Ecru	
▼	Dark brown	869		Background:	
◤	Mid blue	931		Mid green (border)	3052
▽	Light blue	932		Sky blue (border)	3759
✖	Dark green	3051		Deep blue (border)	3750

1740s BEDCHAMBER

This bedchamber has been set in one of the upper rooms of a commercially made dolls' house. Its walls are covered with fabric to the wainscot level (chair rail height) – a practice still popular until about the middle of the eighteenth century when the introduction of wallpapers created new opportunities for decorative treatments. The ceiling, including cornice, and the wall below the chair rail have been painted off-white whilst the floor is cut from a sheet of ready-to-lay miniature floor boarding.

Throughout the Georgian period the massive four-poster bedstead continued to be one of the most important pieces of furniture in the house, dressed now in fabrics in increasingly lavish styles. The four posts of the bed were still tall, supporting a high canopy with roof

This Georgian bedchamber boasts a fabulous four-poster bed which is actually a fairly cheap item that has been transformed by the bed coverings, drapes and pelmet. The chair has also been given a make-over with gilding and a new cover.

often covered with fabrics. Hangings and bed covers ranged from velvet and damasks to light silks and were usually trimmed with gold braid, fringing or tassels. At the beginning of the century bed curtaining still pulled completely around the bed but this fashion was to wane as houses were made warmer and new styles for beds were introduced.

Other furnishings in the room are light, consisting of a beautiful hand-made chest of drawers in burr walnut and a gilded chair with upholstered seat. The bed and chair are readily available, inexpensive pieces which we gilded using a liquid gilding kit. There is a richly coloured rug on the floor which probably would have been knotted wool pile, rather than woven. Early in the century this would have been fairly small as carpets were still expensive.

Soft furnishings in this room comprise a woollen rug, draped bed with coverlet, pelmet and headboard, a chair seat cover and the fabric-covered walls.

✂ FABRIC-COVERED WALLS

Before the development of wallpapers it was a popular practice to cover the walls with fabric, particularly in bedrooms. Perhaps the simplest method of achieving this in miniature is by covering sheets of thin card with material and then gluing these to the walls.(Normally a wainscot or dado rail was positioned about a third of the way up the wall at chair back height to protect the walls from damage by chairs.)

To cover the walls with fabric first measure the distance from the dado rail to the ceiling or just under the cornice, if there is one. This height should be constant around the room. Wall by wall then measure the width, perhaps dividing it into smaller sections to meet at butt joints if there is a door or window to work around. Cut thin card into pieces of the required height by the width. (For a simple room you should have three card panels.) Cut fabric to the dimensions of each card, adding ⅛in extra all round and carefully stretch and fit the fabric by folding it over and gluing it at the back of each card. Do not apply glue to the front of each panel. When dry, fit and glue each covered card into the room, starting with the back wall.

WOOLLEN CARPET

A bedroom of the mid eighteenth century would probably have a richly coloured rug of knotted wool pile over the wooden floor. If you like you can work your own miniature, perhaps using one of the designs in the other Georgian room sets (see pages 36 and 42). Alternatively, buy an upholstery fabric with a suitable pattern to make a rug as we did for the Stuart drawing room (page 28) or photocopy a carpet design onto fabric as we did for the wall hanging in the Elizabethan bedroom (page 21). To give extra weight to the rug scrap fabric can be glued, stitched or bonded to the back.

DRAPED BED WITH COVERLET

Throughout the Georgian period fully draped four-poster beds were still very popular. Ours is a readily available imported version which has had its tail board cut off and the remaining woodwork gilded. There are four main elements to the dressing of this bed which are the bed cover, the side curtains, headboard and canopy façade (bed pelmet). Because this bed can be obtained easily patterns are given for the component parts (pages 49-51) but these may be adapted to fit other makes of bed. To make the mattresses, sheets and pillow refer to the instructions for the Elizabethan bed starting on page 14.

✂ FABRIC BED COVER

To make the bed cover you will need upholstery brocade, Fray Check and multi-purpose glue. Use pattern A (page 49) to cut a piece of upholstery brocade. If the fabric has a design, be it large or small, make sure it is positioned centrally on the bed. Either fray a fringe around the bottom edges of the front and sides or glue or sew on a suitable fringing. To make your own matching fringing cut a strip about ⅛in wide which is long enough to trim the required measurement along both sides and the end of the cover and carefully fray it along one edge until a suitable fringe has been made. Apply liquid Fray Check to prevent further fraying.

Turn back the top edge of the cover (which is to be by the bed head) and the side edges at the foot of the bed which are marked on the pattern by a broken line. These turnings can be either glued, sewn or heat fused using iron-on fusing material such as Bondaweb. Place the finished cover over the mattress and bolster and carefully glue it to the bed frame at the front and sides. We added another cover on top, made to match the drapes. (For details on a similar one see pages 12-13).

CO-ORDINATING BED DRAPES

To make the elegant bed drapes you can either use the same fabric as for the bed cover or choose a different one, as we did. You will need your chosen fabric, lining fabric, matching thread, a Pretty Pleater, thin ribbon or card, glass-headed pins and multi-purpose glue.

Using pattern B on page 50 cut four rectangles 7 x 6in for the side drapes. Use pattern C (page 51) to cut two rectangles 7 x 4in for the end drape. Make the drapes using a Pretty Pleater in the same way as the pleated bed drapes in the Elizabethan bedroom but omit the fringing at the bottom (see page 12). Glue the drapes inside the top canopy frame and to the base where they have a tendency to stick out. You will find that it helps to use glass-headed pins to hold the drapes in the desired position until the glue is dry.

✗ PADDED HEADBOARD

To make this splendid padded headboard for the Georgian bedroom you will need upholstery fabric, thin card, thin foam or cotton wool or tissue and multi-purpose glue.

First make the basic form of the bed head by cutting a piece of thin card and a piece of thin foam, cotton wool or tissue from pattern D on page 51 and gluing the two together. Cut fabric ¼in larger all round using pattern E. Wrap the fabric over the padded side of the card and glue the edges to the back, making sure you do not get any glue on the front. Glue this into the bed head.

✗ BED PELMET

The canopy façade or bed pelmet is the crowning glory of the bed and helps co-ordinate the whole effect by picking up the gold colour of the bed frame. All you need to make it is fabric to match the drapes, gold thread, braid or gift tie, card and glue. No sewing is required.

First cut out the shapes of the side and end pelmets from thin card using patterns F and G (page 50). You will need two of each. Cut two pieces of fabric the same size and two pieces ½in larger all round. Wrap one of the larger pieces of fabric over each card shape, taking the excess to the back and gluing it in place. You will need to snip into the fabric allowances to help it fit neatly into the angles. Glue one of the smaller pieces of fabric over the back of the card, covering the raw fabric edges. To add the trim use a pin or cocktail stick to place glue on the edges of the finished card forms and position thread, fine braid or, as here, gold gift tie on top. Gently ease the finished panels into position and glue them to the top canopy frame.

✗ CHAIR SEAT COVER

Recovering upholstered pieces of less expensive imported furniture is usually a fairly simple operation as these pieces have been designed for ease of manufacture. You will find it is a wonderful way of transforming the pieces and making them co-ordinate better with your room scheme.

Taking an appropriate chair, carefully lift off the seat cushion with the aid of a craft knife. You can now repaint or stain the chair if you wish. In this case the chair was gilded to match the bed. Next remove the existing fabric from the seat cushion as this will provide the pattern for cutting a new piece of fabric. Cut your fabric and simply glue it to the underside of the seat cushion in exactly the same manner as the old one. Be sure not to get any glue on the visible part of the fabric.

For a more elaborate version of re-upholstering an imported piece of furniture see the instructions for the wing chair in the Arts and Crafts parlour, page 89.

Fig. 18 Georgian Bed Set Patterns

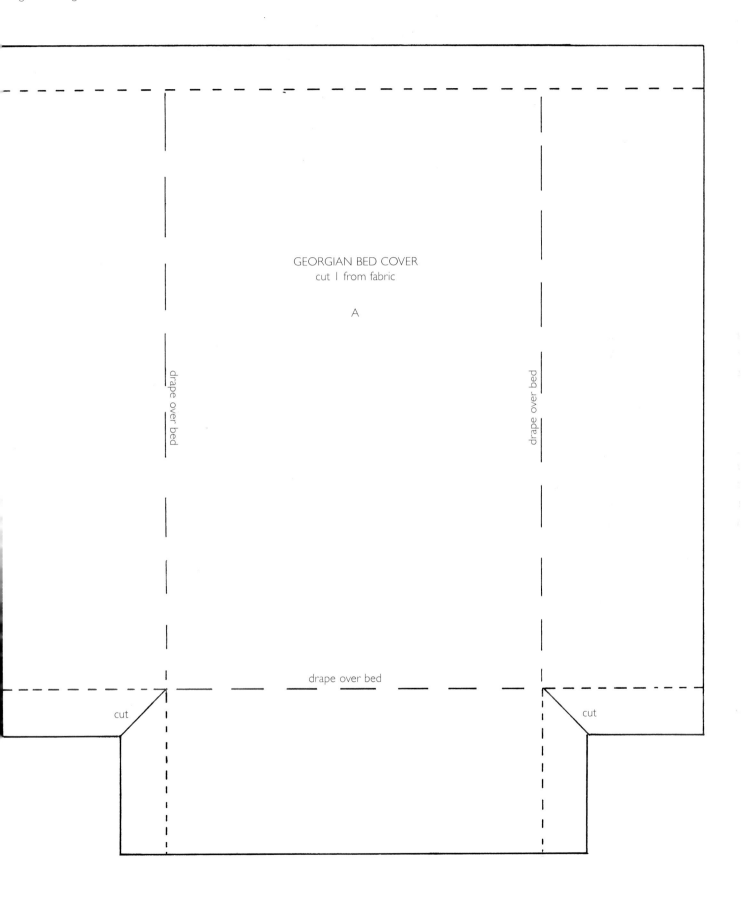

GEORGIAN BED COVER
cut 1 from fabric

A

drape over bed

drape over bed

drape over bed

cut

cut

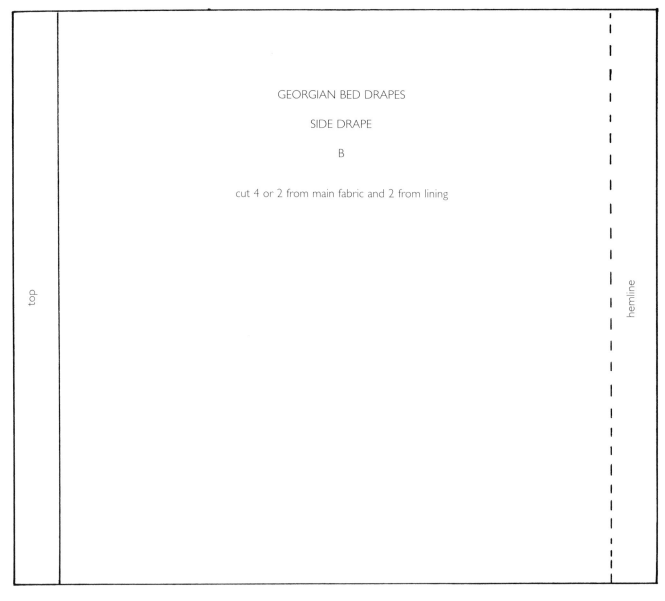

GEORGIAN BED DRAPES

SIDE DRAPE

B

cut 4 or 2 from main fabric and 2 from lining

top

hemline

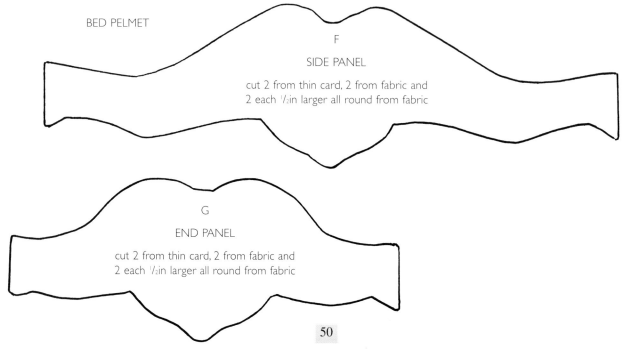

BED PELMET

F

SIDE PANEL

cut 2 from thin card, 2 from fabric and
2 each ½in larger all round from fabric

G

END PANEL

cut 2 from thin card, 2 from fabric and
2 each ½in larger all round from fabric

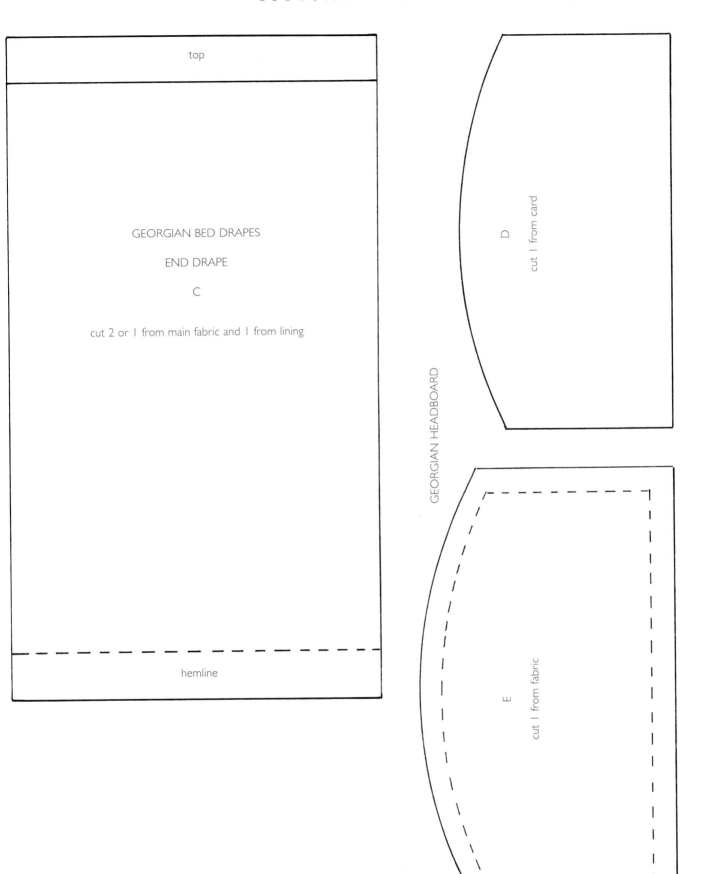

top

GEORGIAN BED DRAPES

END DRAPE

C

cut 2 or 1 from main fabric and 1 from lining

hemline

GEORGIAN HEADBOARD

D

cut 1 from card

E

cut 1 from fabric

REGENCY STYLE

In Britain Regency style was named after the Prince Regent who later became King George IV, while in France the style was termed Empire, in Germany Biedermeier and in the United States American Empire. The Regency period, at its broadest, is considered to be from abo t 1790 ntil the 1830s. This was the time when the notion of interior decoration really came of age. Wallpapers, textiles and carpeting both from home and abroad became m ch more affordable and readily available to the then m ch expanding middle classes. At the same time merchants were only too keen to give advice on decorating trends and there were n mero s p blications on the s bject of interior design now being printed. The Prince Regent was an ardent follower and indeed leader of fashion and b ilt a mon ment to new ideas in interior decorative art in the form of the Royal Pavilion in Brighton.

In essence, within the homes of those who were able to afford the latest look rooms became less formal than previously and ceiling heights lower. Colours used were at the same time lighter and richer, giving a room a much brighter feel. Symmetry within the room was the order of the day with the influence of classicism from early Rome or Greece very much in evidence. To a lesser degree elements of Chinese or Gothic could be found in a number of designed schemes reflecting the romance of an older world. The availability of wall-papers was on the increase and many home owners removed their dado rails in order to show a full drop from ceiling architrave to skirting board. This would often be topped with a paper frieze. Both wallpaper and frieze would be either of a striped or symmetrical design, or a combination of both. Window treatments were particularly fanciful with large amounts of fabric employed for both curtains and top swags and tails.

Carpets too, usually of symmetrical or repeat designs, were now used extensively in more important rooms. These could well be tailor made to fit the room exactly or sometimes fit just short of the walls by about eigh-teen inches. Very often areas of high wear were protected by a plain woven woollen rug known as a drugget. Other soft furnishing used in the room were usually embossed or patterned with designs of urns, vine leaves or other Neo-classical forms as well as the ubiquitous Regency stripe.

REGENCY DINING ROOM

This dining room is decorated in typical Regency style. The furniture is from David Booth while the fender and cornicing are from Sue Cook (see page 165).

This Regency dining room epitomises a style of about 1810-1820. It has striped patterned wallpaper on a pale ground, swagged and tailed curtains at the windows, mahogany furniture and symmetrically placed ornaments representing classical forms. The dining table and chairs are positioned on a plain coloured woollen drugget as often was the practice in dining rooms of this period. A favourite colour, especially for use in dining rooms, was red but much deliberation might go into choosing just the right shade. Here the curtains are of a then fashionable red and the striped chair seats and small patterned wallpaper reflect this same colour. Overall the rich colours of the curtains, the symmetry of the room's arrangement together with the Neo-classicism found in the forms of the mirrors, pictures and accessories combine to make a room which is instantly recognisable as Regency.

This room is 18¾in wide, 12in deep and 10in high and represents realistic dimensions for a room from this period. Probably too large to fit into a conventional dolls' house, this room has been built within an individual room box. However, windows have been cut into the back and the fireplace set into a false wall. Early nineteenth-century style cornice has been glued between wall and ceiling and there is a ceiling rose in the centre of the room. Note the absence of a chair rail around the walls, permitting a continuous run of wallpaper between ceiling and floor. Paintwork is all off-white and the floor is of polished wood strip.

The soft furnishings in this room comprise the pole screen, swagged window treatment, tablecloth, stool and seat covers. We also explain how to make a drugget from a piece of lightweight wool fabric. These were usually in shades of green or brown and were used in poorer homes as substitutes for good carpets or in wealthier households to protect quality carpets from everyday wear. There is also a set of projects – a tapestry seat cover, cushion and co-ordinating footstool – which are not shown in the main room setting. These would suit a blue room scheme but you can easily alter the colours to suit your setting.

REGENCY POLE SCREEN

Changes in fireplaces began to occur in the late eighteenth century with the invention of the Rumford grate. Designed by Benjamin Thompson, an American engineer (a.k.a. Lord Rumford), it replaced the English fireplaces which caused rooms to fill with smoke whilst the heat escaped up the chimney. As Rumford fire grates became more popular in homes throughout Britain fireplace furniture began to appear with such things as coal boxes, pokers, hearth brooms, bellows, bell pulls and, of course, fire screens. Fire screens were either free standing or could be tied to the chair back and were made with painted green silk, rushes or canvas. By the 1830s most homes had this essential piece of furniture.

The 'head' of this free-standing Regency style pole screen has been designed and worked on silk gauze by Sue Bakker and the wood mahogany frame is made by David Booth. To complete the design you will need a round pole screen with an internal measurement of about 1¼in, 48-count silk gauze, a No. 10 embroidery

(crewel) needle, DMC stranded cottons in the colours listed in the key, fine card and glue stick.

Before you begin read the note at the bottom of this page. Use one strand of cotton throughout, working the main design area in half cross stitch and the backgrounds in basketweave stitch (see page 158). Following the chart opposite, begin in the centre at the bird and work outwards. For more advice refer to Using a Chart, page 157. Start working with a 'waste' knot and end by threading the needle through the backs of previous stitches.

To finish, cut a piece of fine card to fit tightly into the well of the round pole screen. Stick the embroidery to the card, being very careful to make sure that the work is centred and precisely vertical. Cut round the outside of the stitching very closely and carefully. Finally, place the mounted embroidery into the hole, gently easing the work under the lip with the blunt end of a needle.

NOTE If you are using a different pole screen to the one shown here by David Booth you will have to measure the opening carefully and adjust the finished circle of the background to fit.

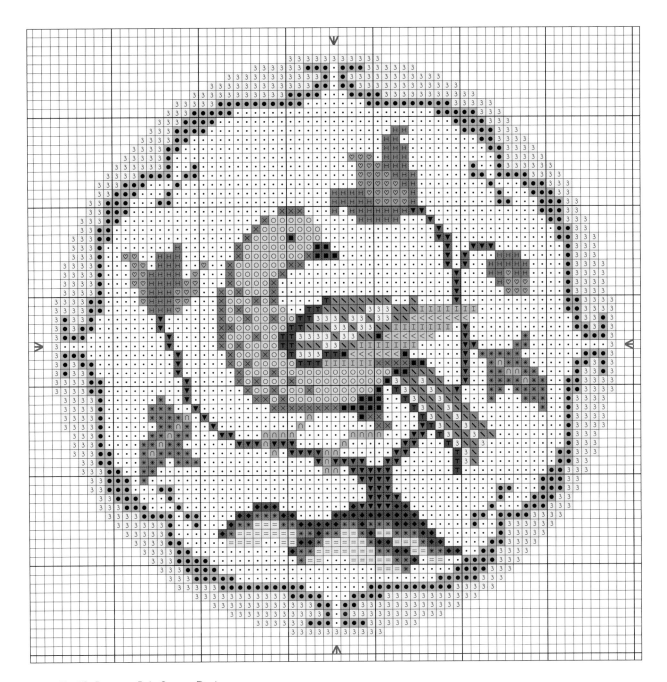

Fig. 19 Regency Pole Screen Design
KEY DMC stranded cotton

BIRD

T	Dark blue	517	■	Dark brown	839
↘	Mid blue	518	✕	Brown	840
3	Light blue	3753			
∩	Pink	3064			
I	Gold	422			
<	Light gold	677			

FLOWERS AND LEAVES

♡	Rose	223
H	Mauve	3041
▼	Grey	646
◆	Dark green	501
✳	Mid green	502
=	Light green	504

BACKGROUND

•	Ecru	841

BORDER

●	Bright gold	729
3	Light blue	3753

⟨X SWAGGED WINDOW TREATMENT

This elegant window treatment with long drapes and swagged valance would have been typical of the period. In the dining room the window treatment was created by Ray Whitledge and is designed so that no sewing is required. To copy it you will need suitable fabric such as velvet or cotton, decorative trim, tassels or cord, fusible webbing material (Bondaweb), a Pretty Pleater, ⅛in wood or acrylic, ½in thick foam core board (polyboard), thin white fabric glue and silk pins. You will also need a curtain pole with finials. Ours was ¾in across and 5in long but you should check the size of your windows.

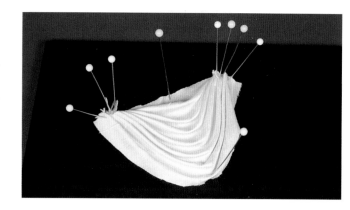

Measure the width of the window and the drop from curtain pole to floor. Add ½in to the width and 1in to the length. For each window cut two pieces of fabric this size (in our case 5½ x 9in). Now cut four pieces of fusible webbing the cut length of each curtain (9in) and ¼in wide and four strips of webbing the cut width of each curtain and ½in wide (½ x 5½in). Fuse one of the wider strips to the bottom of each panel on the wrong side. Fold up the bottom of the curtain by ½in to enclose the webbing and fuse with an iron. Fuse the ¼in strips to each side edge of the curtain on the wrong side, trimming off the excess. Then fold over the fused fabric by ¼in and iron in place as before. Now pleat both panels using the Pretty Pleater (see page 161). Steam several times then allow to cool and dry.

Using pattern A on page 57 (opposite) cut one swag with the arrow on the pattern running along the fabric grain. (For the double swag shown in the picture left, cut two swags.) Fold the swag in half lengthways and snip at ½in intervals as marked on the pattern. Pull each snip up to the top corner to form the swags and pin in place (see above). When all the folds are shaped steam and leave to dry.

Using pattern B on page 57 (opposite) cut a pair of tails or cascades with the fabric grain running from top to bottom. There is no need to cut a lining. Glue decorative trim to the bottom and side edges of each tail using a thin white fabric glue which will also seal the fabric edges. Fold one of the tails like an accordion, either stacked or slightly expanded, following the fold lines which are marked as broken lines on the pattern. Fold the other tail to make a mirror image of the first one then pin the tails to the foam board and steam. Allow to cool and dry.

Draw the area of the window on the foam core board to make a pinning template or guide. Remove the curtains from the pleater and glue the wood/acrylic

This splendid window dressing is an alternative to the single-swag treatment shown in the main room set. It is made in the same way but the swags are hung differently (see right). To co-ordinate with this colourway we have included a set of tapestry seat covers, footstool cover and cushion.

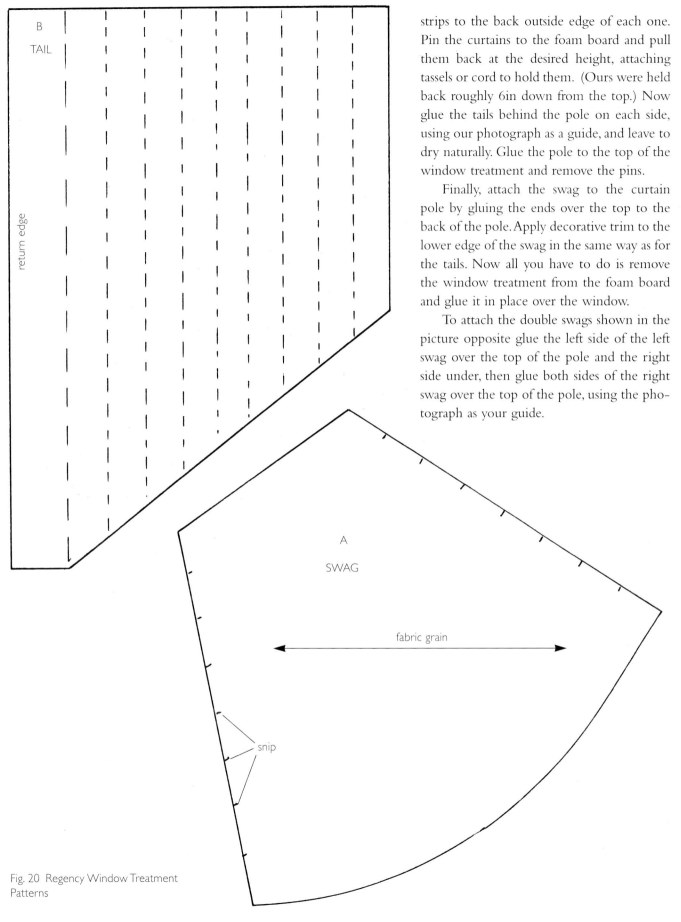

B

TAIL

return edge

A

SWAG

fabric grain

snip

Fig. 20 Regency Window Treatment Patterns

strips to the back outside edge of each one. Pin the curtains to the foam board and pull them back at the desired height, attaching tassels or cord to hold them. (Ours were held back roughly 6in down from the top.) Now glue the tails behind the pole on each side, using our photograph as a guide, and leave to dry naturally. Glue the pole to the top of the window treatment and remove the pins.

Finally, attach the swag to the curtain pole by gluing the ends over the top to the back of the pole. Apply decorative trim to the lower edge of the swag in the same way as for the tails. Now all you have to do is remove the window treatment from the foam board and glue it in place over the window.

To attach the double swags shown in the picture opposite glue the left side of the left swag over the top of the pole and the right side under, then glue both sides of the right swag over the top of the pole, using the photograph as your guide.

OVAL TABLECLOTH

An oval table is a very elegant item of furniture and is ideally suited to this Regency dining room, but it is more difficult to make a cloth for it than for a rectangular table and requires careful cutting and sewing. The best method is to make a pattern first. You will need a suitable fabric – white linen would have been traditional – plus matching fine silk thread, paper, spray starch, kitchen wrap, pins and foam core board (polyboard).

Make your pattern by first drawing around the table top. Then measure the distance from the top of the table to the floor and add this measurement to the oval, all the way round. Add another ½in all round for the hem. Pin the paper pattern to your chosen fabric and cut out with sharp scissors. Machine stitch around the cloth ¼in from the fabric edge. Snip to the stitch line periodically around the hem. This will make the edge curve neatly. Carefully hem by folding over twice, the first time to your stitch line and the second time by the same amount, enclosing the raw edge. Sew the hem in place with fine silk thread. Lightly press when finished.

To dress the table first cover it with a piece of clear kitchen wrap. Stand the table on a piece of foam core board (polyboard) and drape the fabric across the table top. Spray with starch and arrange the table skirt into pleasing folds, pinning the hem to the foam board as you go. When dry, remove the pins and kitchen film and position the table in your miniature setting. Lay the table for an elegant dinner party.

CHAIRS AND STOOL

Our dining chairs from David Booth came beautifully upholstered but if yours need recovering or if you want them to match the room scheme more closely refer to the instructions for the chairs in the Georgian drawing room on page 35 but use the pattern given right. Alternatively, work the beautiful tapestry pattern of stripes and roses as explained here and use this to recover each seat. Our seats suit a blue room scheme but you can easily change the colours as desired. You may also like to work the co-ordinating tapestry cover for the footstool using the pattern shown on page 60 and the matching cushion (see pages 60-61). The cushion and footstool would fit equally well in a bedroom or drawing room and the seat pattern can easily be adapted to fit a chair or set of chairs in another room too.

TAPESTRY CHAIR SEAT

This design by Nicola Mascall is for a set of chair seats suitable for a Regency dining room. The designs are to fit the furniture made by David Booth. The chair seats measure 1⁵⁄₁₆in from front to back, 1¹⁄₁₆in across the back edge and 1⁷⁄₁₆in across the front edge. If you need to change the dimensions to fit another chair make sure you keep the centre stripe central and increase or reduce evenly all the way round the existing chart.

To make the set of seat covers you will need 48 hpi silk gauze, Mulberry silk twist in the colours given in the key, a size 26 tapestry needle and cardboard to make a mount. You will also need foam or felt padding, card and multi-purpose glue to mount the seat.

Begin by mounting the silk gauze on cardboard which has a window in it slightly larger than the area to be sewn (see page 156). Use masking tape to attach the gauze to the card, keeping the weave of the fabric square with the edges of the card and keeping the gauze as taut as possible. Mark the top of the mount for reference. Each square on the chart represents one square or mesh of the silk gauze.

Use two strands of silk throughout, working the design in half cross stitch. (If you have difficulty separating the strands of silk, simply wet your fingers and untwist the thread.) Limit the length of the thread to about 10in to help prevent knotting and fluffing. Following the chart opposite, begin by working the central stripe first, then work out to the edges, leaving the darkest shades until last. Use half cross stitch (see page 158), For more advice, refer to Using a Chart, page 157. When the design is finished carefully remove the masking tape and lift it off the cardboard mount. Iron the work with the wrong side up, using a pressing cloth.

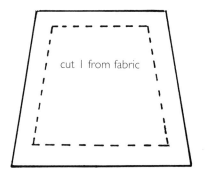

Fig. 21 Regency Chair Seat Pattern

Cut a card form on which to mount the finished tapestry, making it a little smaller than the chair recess to allow for the bulk of the fabric. You will find this easier if you use paper to make a pattern first. Cut a piece of

padding – foam, felt or similar – to the same size as the card form. Now place the needlepoint face down on a clean work surface and centre first the padding and then the card on top. Use white multi-purpose glue to stick

Fig 22 Striped Chair Seat Cover Design

KEY   Mulberry silk twist

·	Ecru	W50	O	Mid blue	W434	✚	Mid gold	W7	L	Pale green	W977	◨	Dark green	W398
●	Pale blue	W433	△	Pale gold	W488	✚✚	Dark gold	W413	↗	Mid green	W397			

the front and back edges of the work to the back of the card. Check that the edges of the work are even at the front and back and that no unstitched gauze is showing on the right side. Also check that the seat fits back into the chair and adjust if necessary. Glue the side edges in place, applying the glue to the card, rather than the gauze. As before, check the fit of the cover in the chair before the glue sets completely, then set aside to dry. When dry, fit the seat into the chair with glue around the edges on the bottom of the seat cover.

⊠ CO-ORDINATING FOOTSTOOL

This tapestry cover is the perfect complement to the chair seats, but if you prefer you can simply cover the footstool in upholstery fabric, carefully unpeeling the old cover and using it as a guide for the new cover (see below). To work the tapestry you will need the same materials as for the chair seat but use a size 28 tapestry needle. You will also need thin cotton fabric for backing.

First measure the width of the stool because you may need to extend or reduce the edges of the pattern to fit. The 28 rows on the chart (from top to bottom) must be repeated until the piece is long enough to fit your footstool. Work it in exactly the same manner as the chair seat

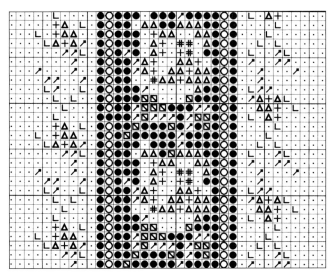

Fig. 23 Tapestry Footstool Design

KEY   Mulberry silk twist

·	Ecru	W50		⊞	Dark gold	W413
●	Pale blue	W433		L	Pale green	W977
○	Mid blue	W434		⟋	Mid green	W397
△	Pale gold	W488		◨	Dark green	W398
⊞	Mid gold	W7				

covers, starting in the centre and working outwards. Where possible, work the paler shades first to avoid darker colours showing through.

When the design is complete carefully remove the tapestry from the cardboard mount. Iron it with the wrong side up using a pressing cloth to protect it. Cut a piece of thin cotton fabric the required finished size for the footstool. Place this on the reverse side of the work and fold the long side edges of the tapestry over it. Lightly glue the unstitched edges of the tapestry to the fabric. Repeat at top and bottom. Now glue the tapestry onto the footstool.

⊠ TAPESTRY CUSHION

If you have made the seat and footstool covers by Nicola Mascall you may like to make this cushion too which is designed to match the set. You will need 48 hpi silk gauze, Mulberry silk twist, a size 26 tapestry needle and fine crewel needle, backing fabric, ecru thread, rice or salt for stuffing, and cardboard.

Begin by mounting the silk gauze on a cardboard frame as for the tapestry chair seat. Each square on the chart represents one square or mesh of the silk gauze. Use two strands of silk throughout, working the design in half cross stitch (see page 158). Where possible, work the background areas in basketweave stitch which causes less distortion of the canvas. (See the tapestry chair seat, page 58 and Using a Chart, page 157, for further advice.) Following the chart opposite, begin by working the central stripe first, then work out to the edges, leaving the darkest shades until last.

When the design is complete carefully remove the tapestry from the cardboard mount. Iron it with the wrong side up using a pressing cloth to protect it. Then trim the gauze to approximately ¼in around the work, leaving the bottom edge a little larger. Cut a piece of backing fabric slightly larger than the trimmed tapestry and pin them together with right sides facing and the tapestry centred. Beginning at the lower right-hand corner of the design, backstitch around three sides using a fine crewel needle and ecru thread and taking small stitches. Keep to the very edge of the design and make sure the backing fabric is kept straight.

Trim neatly around the three sides, leaving just a small seam allowance, then snip a little triangle of fabric off the top two corners. Carefully turn the cushion the

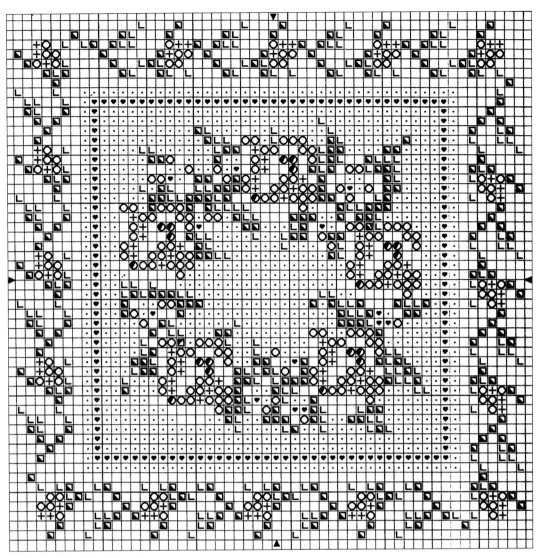

Fig. 24 Tapestry Cushion Design

KEY Mulberry silk twist

☐	Cream	W609
·	Pale blue	W433
♥	Mid blue	W434
○	Pale gold	W488
+	Mid gold	W7
◑	Dark gold	W413
L	Mid green	W397
◪	Dark green	W398

right way out, fill with salt or rice and close the gap by tucking in the seam allowances and slipstitching the seam closed. To finish make a cord by twisting three 20in long strands of silk together and stitch the cord to the seam in the same way as for the Orchard Floor Cushion in the Stuart drawing room (page 29).

✕ SIMPLE DRUGGET

Druggets were very basic, plain floor coverings made from heavy-duty materials such as baize, serge or hair-cloth. They were used specifically to protect Axminster or Wilton carpets from dirt and wear, to catch crumbs in dining rooms, falling soot from chimneys, or hair powder in dressing rooms – wherever there was heavy wear. In wealthier households when a fine carpet was

ordered a drugget would always be included alongside in shades of either green or brown. When the drugget was removed for guests it indicated just how important the visitors were. Poorer households used druggets as substitutes for good carpets as they were not only inexpensive but very hard wearing and made rooms look neat and comfortable. Sometimes druggets were edged with a border of needlework which made the plain cloth more interesting.

Our drugget is 12 x 8in but you can make it any size. You will need a piece of lightweight wool fabric in either brown or green cut to the required finished size plus Fray Check or iron-on backing such as interfacing. Unless already non-fray, treat the fabric with Fray Check or apply iron-on backing, then position in the room. The drugget should lie flat with no difficulty.

CHINESE STYLE MORNING ROOM

An interest in the Orient – or more specifically anything Chinese – had a great influence on interior design at the beginning of the nineteenth century and no less because of the chinoiserie styles incorporated in the interiors of the Royal Pavilion at Brighton. Just how experimental Regency decorators could be is shown in the wide variety of bright colours used within the room, particularly with the colour purple. The walls are covered in a rich paper with a Chinese design and the floor is carpeted from wall to wall. Further Chinese influences can be found in the two side tables, the ceramic ginger jars and the bowl on a table behind the chaise longue.

The soft furnishings in the room comprise the upholstered chaise longue with bolster, the elaborate window drapes with double pelmet, the chair seat cover for a metal kit chair, the two fireside floor cushions and the fitted fabric carpet.

CURTAINS WITH DOUBLE PELMET

The lavish curtains in front of the French doors in this room are made from a deep purple and gold fabric – a bold move but very much in keeping with the ideas of the day. The French doors are 6½in wide which is wider than a standard window and each curtain must be made this width to give the necessary fullness. Make both curtains and the swags in the same way as the curtains in the Regency dining room (page 56), making two swags from the pattern given. You do not need the tails. Mount the curtains on the pole as instructed and then glue on the swags, placing them side by side as shown in the picture. To make the tiebacks cut two strips of fabric the desired size and bond backing fabric, such as iron-on interfacing, to the back to prevent fraying. Alternatively, use cord tiebacks in the same way as for the dining room.

SIDE CHAIR

Lacquered furniture is an essential part of the Chinese decorative style so we felt it was important to include at least one item in our room set. The single chair featured here was made from a metal kit which came with no padded seat. To make a seat cushion for a chair like this

simply cut out a thin piece of card to the dimensions of the seat area, pad it with cotton wool, foam or tissue and cover with fabric in the same way as the Regency dining chairs (see page 58). You will find it easier if you make a paper pattern of the seat first.

CHAISE LONGUE WITH BOLSTER

The chaise longue is an elegant piece of furniture which became popular in the nineteenth century. Although designed for reclining on, the padding on the back and seat was minimal to retain the smooth, clean lines which were popular at the time, so bolsters or cushions were a necessity if any comfort was to be enjoyed. Our chaise longue came beautifully upholstered from David Booth and perhaps it should not be

recommended that this delicate piece be recovered. However, should it be absolutely necessary re-upholstery is possible although great care is needed, particularly in the removal of the existing fabric. In addition to your new fabric you will need braid and glue.

To recover the chaise longue first carefully unpeel the outside end panel and the decorative braid that runs around to the front of the piece. Next lift off the main seat cushion, the outside head panel, the inside head and tail panels, the back braid, the back outside panel and finally the back cushion. Cut out new fabric pieces following patterns A-G on page 64, taking care to match the fabric pattern repeats, if appropriate. Recover and refit each component part in the reverse order of removal, either reusing or replacing the braid as you go. (For further advice see the instructions for recovering

This morning room has been created using miniature components produced by Sue Cook. These include the fireplace and Regency chinoiserie overmantle, the columns, the cornicing and the matching ceiling rose. The central chandelier was made by Phyllis Tucker.

the Chippendale style sofa and chair seats in the Georgian drawing room, page 35.)

To make the bolster simply dismantle the existing one and use the removed pieces as patterns to cut new pieces. Sew the joining sides of the main rectangle together with backstitch, leaving a gap in the centre for stuffing. Snip into the seam allowances of the ends at intervals for ease, then pin the two circular end pieces in place and stitch. Turn the cover out through the gap and stuff quite firmly with rice or salt. Slipstitch the gap closed with the smallest stitches you can manage.

Fig. 25 Chaise Longue Cover Patterns

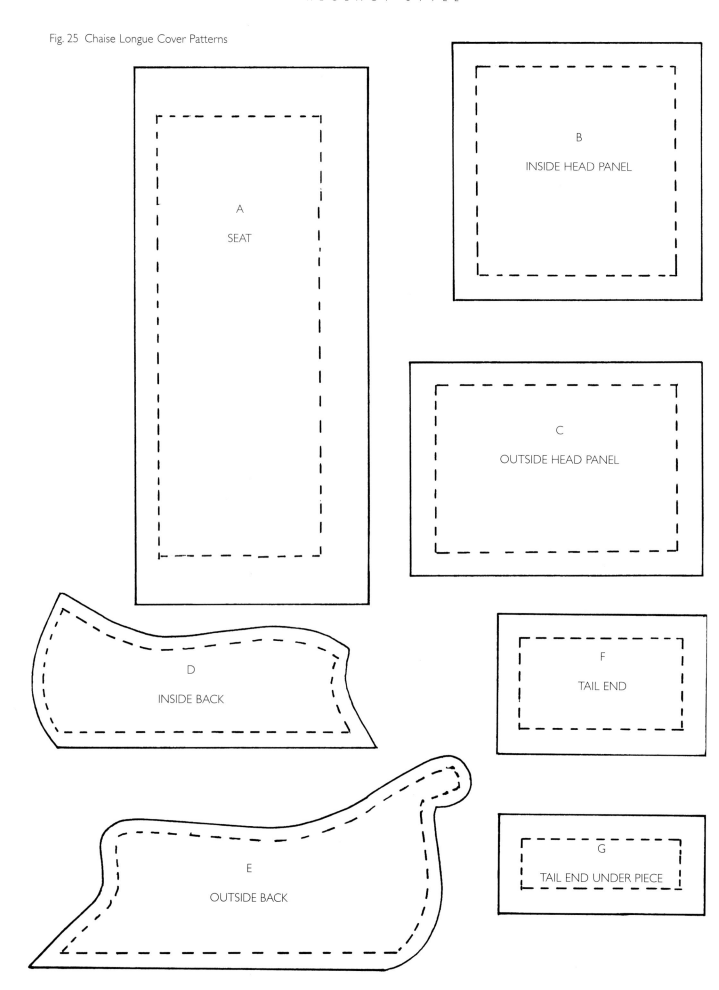

A
SEAT

B
INSIDE HEAD PANEL

C
OUTSIDE HEAD PANEL

D
INSIDE BACK

F
TAIL END

E
OUTSIDE BACK

G
TAIL END UNDER PIECE

 FITTED CARPET

By 1810 the fitting of broad-loom carpets wall to wall had gained popularity. For us, working in miniature, this is perhaps an easier look to achieve than it might be in real life. You will need a suitable piece of fabric – upholstery or curtain fabrics often make good carpeting – plus pins and glue.

Cut the fabric to the exact dimensions of the room before the skirting boards have been fitted. Trial fit the fabric in the room and carefully cut around any pillars, fireplaces and so on. It may be necessary to make a small allowance to turn the fabric under where, for example, there might be a fireplace hearth or at the front edge of the room. Press any turnings with an iron then carefully glue the carpet around the edge of the room, making sure that not too much glue is applied which might seep through. Pin the fabric through to the underfloor to help secure the carpet until the glue dries. When dry fit the skirting boards to the wall above the carpet. This should disguise the raw edges of the fabric.

 FLOOR STOOLS

These simple floor stools with tasselled ends are deceptively easy to make and add to the oriental feel in the room. For each one you will need ¾in thick wood or

foam, fabric, thin card and multi-purpose glue plus four small tassels (see the Georgian curtain tassels, page 34).

Cut a block of wood or foam 1½ x 1½ x ¾in using pattern A below. From fabric cut two pieces from pattern B and one piece from pattern C. From thin card cut a strip 6 x ¾in. Fold fabric piece B over the top of the block and the other piece over the bottom and glue at the sides. Now wrap the strip of fabric around the card and fold the long edges to the back, gluing them in place. Finally, glue this covered strip around the block until it butt joins on one side. Glue in place then trim the corners with small tassels as shown in the photograph.

Fig. 26 Floor Stool Patterns

A

STOOL

cut 1 from ³/₄in wood or foam

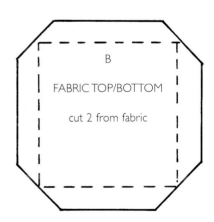

B

FABRIC TOP/BOTTOM

cut 2 from fabric

C
FABRIC SIDES
cut 1 from fabric

REGENCY SALON

This room would have been found within a very grand house indeed. The massive fireplace measures nearly 5in high, which is five foot in real terms, and 7in wide. Obviously it would require a fairly large room to accommodate it. The wallpaper with frieze, ceiling cornice, fireplace, overmantle mirror and general colouring is typical of the Regency style. So too is the furniture in the form of a side cabinet with grilled front, the sabre-legged chair and the circular table with brass trim from Tarbena, and the elegant sewing table and sofa.

Lighting in the room is still by candle which presented quite a job for household servants who had to light and trim the candle wicks. This scene probably represents only one end of a larger room and there could well be another matching chandelier at the other end. It was intended that light should also be reflected in the huge mirror above the fireplace. This fine miniature chandelier, together with the crystal candlesticks on the fireplace, were made by specialist Phyllis Tucker.

Notice the paintings on the walls. Popular subjects for pictures at this time were either landscape scenes or family portraits. Ornaments or objects decorating the room reflect classical lines and are provided by urns and figurines. The ceiling and other paintwork is off-white while the floor is of stained boarding, this time covered with a woven carpet that finishes about eighteen inches short of the walls.

Soft furnishings in this room comprise the carpet, sofa cover and chair.

The proportions of this salon show that this is a room in a large house. Furnishings are traditional but still reflect true Regency style. The lady in 1820s costume was made and dressed by Jill Bennett.

Fig. 27 Regency Sofa Patterns

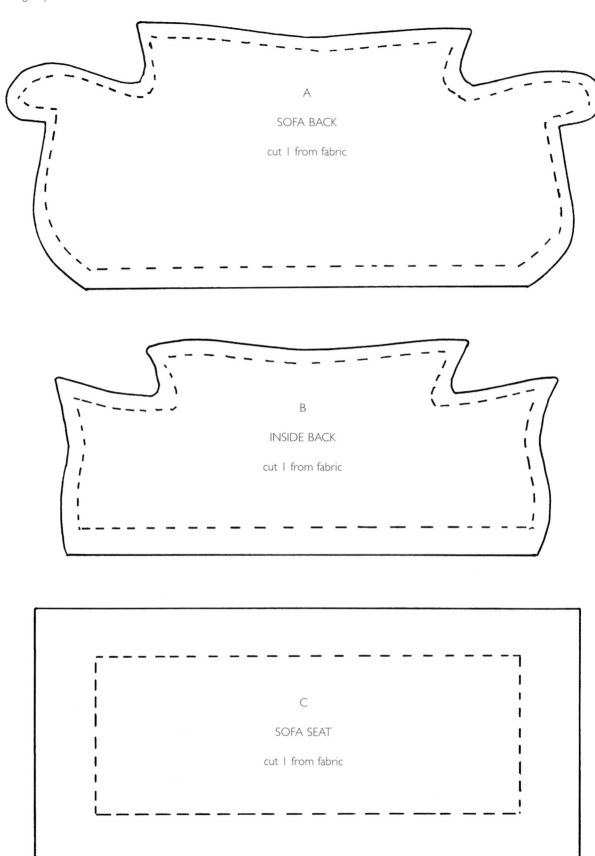

A

SOFA BACK

cut 1 from fabric

B

INSIDE BACK

cut 1 from fabric

C

SOFA SEAT

cut 1 from fabric

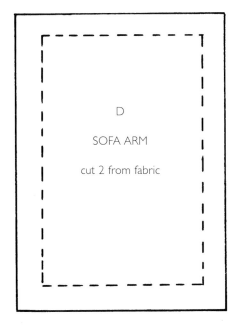

D

SOFA ARM

cut 2 from fabric

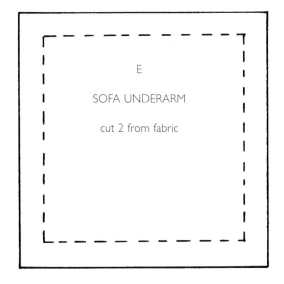

E

SOFA UNDERARM

cut 2 from fabric

✕ REGENCY CHAIR

The chair in the salon was produced by Tarbena. If required, the seat pattern can be carefully unglued for re-upholstery. All you need is your chosen fabric and some multi-purpose glue.

With this chair or any similar version use the existing pad as a pattern to cut fabric of your choice, adding about 3/16in all round and centring any pattern neatly. Lay out the fabric, wrong side up, and centre the pad face down on top. Fold the excess fabric over the pad around the edges and glue in place, paying special attention to

corners to ensure a neat finish and trimming off the excess fabric here as necessary. Carefully fit the seat pad back in the chair.

✕ REGENCY STYLE SOFA

The normal Regency sofa made by David Booth is almost impossible to recover so he has designed a kit version specially for this project which is still available upon request. (For contact details see Resources and Address Book on page 165.) From fabric simply cut out the pieces given left and above, making sure that any pattern will match where the pieces meet. Carefully cover the sofa in the same way as for the chaise longue in the Chinese room (page 62). Start by fitting the inside back, then the outside back followed by the arms, then the underarms and finally the sofa seat.

✕ REGENCY CARPET

As well as wall to wall carpets in the Regency period a popular style was to finish the carpet about 18in from the wall in order to show a portion of the floorboards. To achieve this look take the dimensions of your miniature room and cut a piece of suitable fabric 1in narrower and 1in shorter. This will allow ½in on each edge for turnings. Turn the ½in allowance under, cutting off any overlap at the corners and secure with either a simple stitch, glue or heat bonding medium. Press and fit in your room setting.

VICTORIAN STYLE

From the end of the eighteenth century and well into the nineteenth a major Industrial Revolution was taking place. As a result of developments in manufacturing machinery, goods became more plentiful and affordable. Lace, now made by machine rather than by hand, became hugely popular and covered any and every otherwise unadorned surface in the home. Woven patterned fabrics, produced on jacquard looms, also became popular and were used for all manner of window treatments as well as to dress archways, doors, mirrors and even the fireplace mantel. The notable exception was the bed – it was thought unhealthy to sleep surrounded by curtaining and fabric bed canopies so the ornate bed treatments of the past died out.

❋　　❋　　❋

With their new-found wealth, sections of the middle classes could afford to build and furnish homes which revealed their status, education and taste to all. They filled their homes with every conceivable furnishing or *objet d'art* that would reflect their new ideals and impress the visitor, from vases and figurines to plants and pictures, books and other paraphernalia. Initially colours for soft furnishings and wall coverings were comparatively sombre, partly for practicality to hide dirt left by the famous London smog. However, with the development of synthetic colour dyes in the mid nineteenth century interiors often became a profusion of bright or garish colours with patterns and contrasting

In keeping with the mid Victorian look the furnishings in this room are many and varied. They include pieces from Escutcheon, Edwardian Elegance, Phoenix Models and '9'. Pictures, books, clock and ornaments also come from different sources but the oil lamp and chandelier are by Ray Storey Lighting. The gentleman was dressed by specialist Sue Atkinson.

colours. Generally, however, throughout the Victorian era the homes of the middle and wealthy classes were decorated in dark tones of greens, reds, browns and sometimes blue for both soft furnishings and the now popular wallpapers. Furniture was plentiful and ornamentation abundant. Favoured soft furnishing materials were velvets, wools, brocades and damasks, with the popularity of printed cottons growing towards the end of the era.

Furniture was bulky and where applicable well upholstered, cushioned and trimmed. It appeared in many forms even within the same room. However, from about 1860 until the early 1900s the middle class desire for an over furnished interior decreased as many women tired of the home pursuits of embroidery, needlework and the like and longed for life outside their imprisoning homes. As is often the case there was a backlash against designs produced by the machine age and a wish to return to older, hand crafted arts and crafts. Methods of production for these remained expensive so by and large homes decorated in the Arts and Crafts style belonged mostly to the well to do or aesthetically aware.

MID VICTORIAN GENTLEMAN'S STUDY

This gentleman's study would date around 1857 and it is part of our Gothic Villa, now supplied by Anglesey Dolls' Houses. The original model of this dolls' house, conceived by Sue and Trevor Cook, has architectural features and aspects of design taken from real buildings dating from the latter part of the eighteenth century. Gothic styling enjoyed an early Victorian revival so such a house might well have been considered very up to date.

This room is 11½in wide, 13½in deep and 8¾in high and we have created our own side window in the wall towards the back. Around the ceiling we used a mid eighteenth century style cornice and stained standard wood mouldings for the skirting board and picture rail. To match we also stained the Gothic style door and surround. The wallpaper is a hand-blocked pattern once available from Small Interiors and the floor is cut from a sheet of boarding.

Soft furnishings made for this room comprise the carpet, various table mats, the mantle cover, bell pull, curtains, cushions, chair and bench covers and the sofa which is made from balsa wood and card.

STUDY CARPET

The finished carpet for this room is 9½ x 8¼in. To make one simply follow the instructions for the carpet in the Regency salon, page 69. We used an even heavier upholstery fabric to make this one so it was important to trim the folds at the corners when we turned the ⅛in hem allowances under.

CURTAINS

Victorian curtains were usually made from traditional curtaining fabrics such as velvet, and they might be plain or patterned. However, although the fabrics were the same, their colours and patterns were changing in line with the new fashions while designs were simplifying. Generally colours were fairly dark, with green, red, brown or blue as popular choices. The ornate pelmets of the Georgian era were now gone and simple paired curtains were popular. This was probably because Victorian homes tended to have lower ceilings and pelmets would have cut out the light and made the windows look smaller.

Here we have hung floor-length curtains from a pole. The fabric is patterned but the design and colours are fairly masculine in keeping with the look of a gentleman's study. To make them you will need cotton velvet, matching thread, fusible bonding fabric (Bondaweb), a Pretty Pleater, spray starch, glue and a curtain pole.

Measure the drop from the curtain pole to the floor and the width of the window. Cut two pieces of fabric to this measurement, adding 1in to the length for hems, then assemble the curtains in the same way as the velvet curtain in the Stuart drawing room (see page 28).

MANTLE COVER

The idea of covering fireplace mantles was a popular notion, very much in keeping with the Victorian's ideal of embellishing absolutely everything. Our mantle cover was designed by Sue Cook, and we have included the pattern on page 75. Check the fit on your fireplace and extend it as necessary.

This close-up of the study fireplace shows the mantle cover. Notice how the fabric pattern has been carefully centred. Our cover is made from fabric-covered card. The card gives body and helps the fabric lie flat. The braid is optional but gives a neat finish.

Cut piece A from thin card and piece B from fabric, making sure you arrange the fabric pattern appropriately. Lay out your fabric wrong side up and position the card on top. Glue the fabric overlap allowances onto the card and leave to dry. Then fold the finished piece over along the broken lines on the pattern and glue together at the corners, if necessary. Add a trim of fringing or braid around the bottom if extra decoration is required.

MID VICTORIAN SOFA

The plans for this Victorian style sofa are very similar to those printed in women's journals and the like of the late 1800s for instructing children on making furniture for their dolls' houses. Although not very detailed it certainly has an authentic touch. To make it you will need ¼in

thick balsa wood, medium-weight card, suitable upholstery fabric, ¼in thick foam or other padding material, wood for the legs, multi-purpose glue, thick matching thread and a braid trim.

Using the patterns in Fig. 29 first cut the seat (B) from ¼in balsa wood and the back (A) from medium-weight card. To ease the back around the curved base it is a good idea to cut the fabric which will cover this piece on the bias. Cut two pieces of fabric from pattern A but add ¼in all round one piece and ½in all round the other. Cut pattern C from fabric to go round the front of the sofa and pattern B for the seat, this time adding about ½in all round each piece. Cut two pieces of ¼in thick foam or other padding material from patterns A and B.

Fit the fabric seat front (C) to the front edge of the balsa sofa base by folding the ½in seam allowance back all

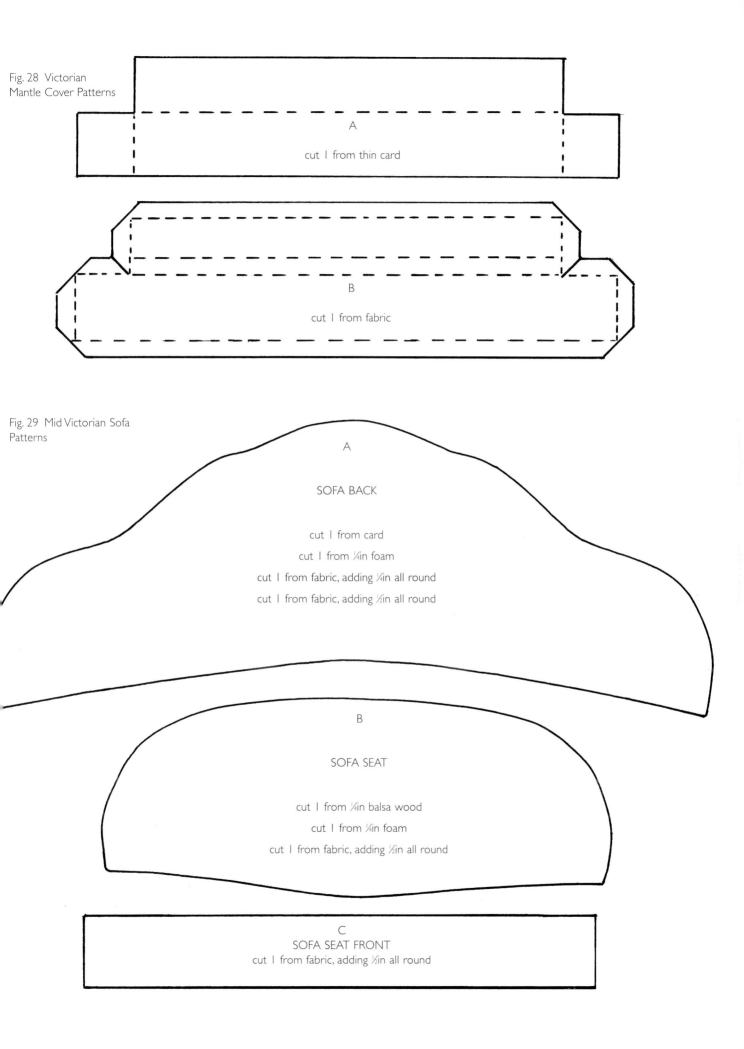

Fig. 28 Victorian
Mantle Cover Patterns

A

cut 1 from thin card

B

cut 1 from fabric

Fig. 29 Mid Victorian Sofa
Patterns

A

SOFA BACK

cut 1 from card

cut 1 from ¼in foam

cut 1 from fabric, adding ¼in all round

cut 1 from fabric, adding ½in all round

B

SOFA SEAT

cut 1 from ¼in balsa wood

cut 1 from ¼in foam

cut 1 from fabric, adding ½in all round

C
SOFA SEAT FRONT
cut 1 from fabric, adding ½in all round

When dry, use thick thread to make French knots (see page 159) at about ½in intervals over the back to create a Victorian style buttoned effect. Glue this finished piece into the back of the sofa, enclosing the seam allowances of the covered card back. For the seat cushion follow the same procedure, French knotting buttons only if desired.

From wood, either straight section or turned, fashion four (or six) legs ¾in long and glue them to the underside of the sofa. Finally, glue or sew a braid trim around the top and front edges or, for an alternative look, add a larger fringing of plain fabric about 1in deep around the base to form a skirt. (To make your own fringing see the instructions for the fabric bed cover in the Georgian bedroom, page 47.)

BUTTONED CHAIR SEAT

Victorian style metal chairs in kit form are readily available and are ideal for many room sets, including a study like this one. Before you assemble the kit you can upholster the seat to give it a more comfortable look. All you need is a drill with a fine drill bit, fabric, multi-purpose glue and matching stranded embroidery cotton (floss).

Use the fine drill to make holes in the seat where buttons are indicated. Next cut a piece of fabric that will fold over the chair seat top to the underside, making sure any pattern is arranged carefully. Dab glue around the underside of the seat then place the fabric on the seat and fold the edges to the underside, making sure the fabric fits as tightly as it can. Cut away any surplus fabric from the underside for a neat finish. With one strand of stranded cotton make French knots (see page 159) on the top of the seat to represent buttoning, pulling the thread to the underside. Work from one hole to the next, making French knots in each before tying off underneath.

BENCH SEAT CUSHION

The bench seat on the right hand wall of the study has the solid, dark Gothic look which was so popular with the Victorians. This one (produced by '9') has a comfortable seat cushion and co-ordinating squab cushions (see below) to make it more inviting. To make the seat cushion all you need is ⅛in thick balsa wood, sandpaper, suitable fabric and multi-purpose glue.

Cut a piece of balsa wood to fit comfortably onto the seat of the bench then smooth round the edges of

round and then gluing these folded sections to the top and sides of the base. Leave the bottom edge free. Next take the fabric piece A with the ¼in allowances and cover the back of the card sofa back, bringing the extra ¼in allowance to the front and gluing it down. When dry glue the bottom edge of the covered card to the back and sides of the sofa base, temporary pinning it with glass-headed pins to help force the card is into shape. Be sure that both the base and the back are flush with the underside of the seat.

Cover the foam piece A with the remaining back fabric, turning the allowances to the back and gluing them in place. (Trim off ¼in at the bottom if necessary.)

the 'cushion' with sandpaper, paying extra attention to the front. Cut a piece of fabric ¾in larger all round than the top face of the balsa block and wrap it around the block, gluing the allowances on the bottom and keeping the corners in shape by stretching the fabric round them. When the glue has dried fit the cushion in place.

SQUAB CUSHIONS

We made two large squab cushions for the bench from old pieces of fabric taken from a full-sized nineteenth century pieced patchwork cushion cover. To make a similar cushion you will need a suitable fabric, matching thread and rice or salt for the filling.

Cut two pieces of fabric approximately 1½in square. Pin them together with right sides facing and hand sew all round with running stitch or backstitch, taking a small seam allowance and leaving a gap for turning and filling. Turn the cushion right side out, fill with rice or salt and then close the gap with slipstitch.

RIBBONS AND ROSES BELL PULL

Servants were common in Victorian times in most upper and middle class households, even if there was just a cook, gardener and an upstairs maid, so bell pulls were widely used. The one shown overleaf is an original design by Nicola Mascall and features a pretty floral design on a swirl of ribbon. You will need 40 hpi silk gauze, a size 26 tapestry needle, Madeira stranded embroidery cotton (floss) in the colours in the key, cardboard, glue, a piece of leather for backing and a brass hanging ring.

Begin by mounting the silk gauze on firm card with a window cut in the card slightly larger than the area to be sewn. Use masking tape to secure the gauze, keeping the weave of the fabric square with the edges of the card and keeping the gauze as taut as possible (see page 156).

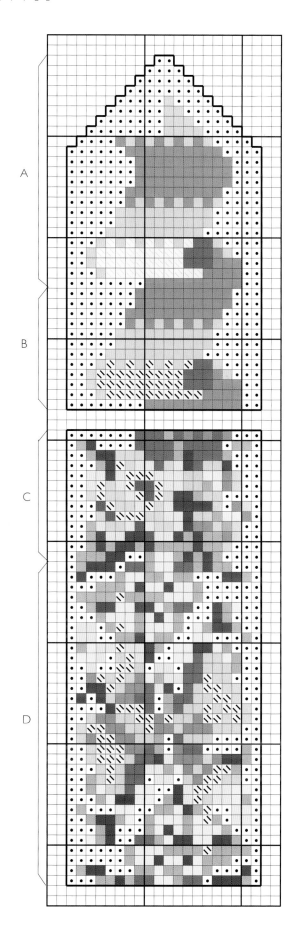

Fig. 30 Ribbons and Roses Bell Pull Design
KEY   Madeira stranded cotton

■ Dark pink	0810	▨ Mid blue	1711
□ Mid pink	0812	▨ Dark blue	1712
▨ Light pink	0813	□ Light gold	2208
■ Dark green	1508	▨ Dark gold	2210
▨ Light green	1510	◨ Ecru	2404
▨ Light blue	1710	• Black	2400

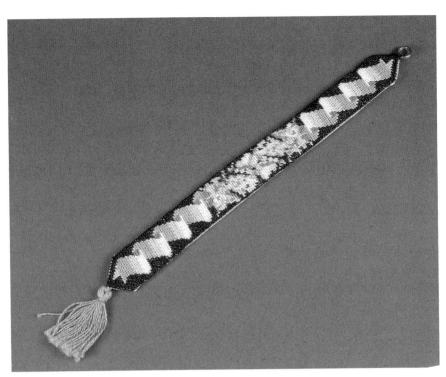

Mark the top of the mount for reference. Each square on the chart represents one square or mesh of the silk gauze. Using two strands of cotton throughout, work the piece in half cross stitch, following the chart given right. Begin at the top point of the design and work sections A and B of the chart. It is easiest to work the colours in the order in which they appear on the chart. Work the background colour last to avoid the dark colour showing through. Repeat the twelve rows of section B only twice more, then continue with sections C and D.

Now turn the work around so that the bottom becomes the top and work section C again, but this time, begin at the bottom row (row 13) to complete the flowers and remainder of the centre section of the design. Keeping the work the same way round, work section B in the same manner (beginning at row 12 of the section). Repeat twice more. Finally, work section A to complete the pattern. Fill in the black background.

Remove the completed design from the cardboard mount and carefully iron it with the wrong side up, using a pressing cloth to protect it. Trim the long sides to approximately ¼in following the weave of the gauze, then trim the top and bottom edges in the same way. With the wrong side up turn over the corners on each side of the top and bottom ends like a mitred corner, creating a point at the end and oversew the vertical hems together. Now fold over the long sides, following the edge of the

embroidery. The edges of the gauze should just about meet down the centre. Lightly press on the wrong side. Make and attach a tassel on the end and attach a brass ring to the top by oversewing four or five times with black thread.

Back the bell pull with a leather strip cut into a long strip the length of the pull and about ½in wide, or just a fraction narrower than the bell pull. Cut the ends of the leather into a 'V' shape to match the 'V' of the finished bell pull. Spread glue on the back of the finished tapestry and attach the leather very carefully.

SILK TABLE RUNNER

An elegant table runner adorns the table beside the fireplace which has been specially hand woven for us by Bonni Backe. If you have weaving skills you can make it following the instructions given here. The runner is 1¹¹⁄₁₆in wide and 4⅝in long but it can be easily extended to suit your piece of furniture. If you do not have weaving skills, make a runner from a piece of woven upholstery fabric, fraying the edges to make a fringe in the same way as the table runner at the Tudor Feast (see pages 25–26). You will need two yards of silk for this runner.

For the warp use 160/2 silk with 127 ends, sleyed 4 per dent in a No. 17 reed for 68 epi – ⅛in in the reed. For the weft use 160/2 silk 60ppi. Thread as follows:

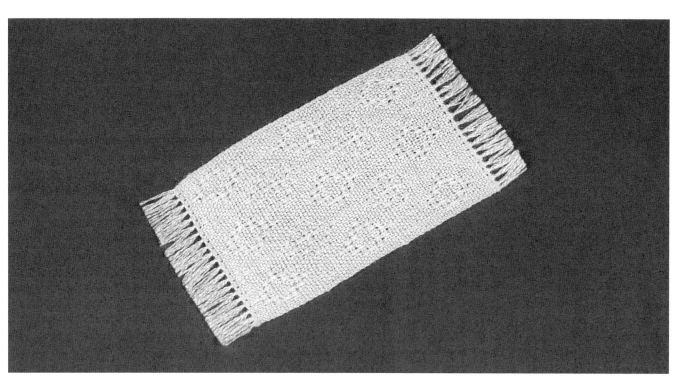

(1, 2) x 5 for selvedge, then A, B, C, D, E, F, E, D, C, B, A, B, C, D, E, F, E, D, C, B, A, ending with (1, 2) x 5 and doubling the outside ends.

KEY
A = 2, 3, 2, 3, 2
B = 1, 4, 1, 4, 1
C = 2, 5, 2, 5, 2
D = 1, 6, 1, 6, 1
E = 2, 7, 2, 7, 2
F = 1, 8, 1, 8, 1

This draw may be woven into runners with a narrow band of tuck lace borders on each end or in an all-over diamond pattern. The fringe should be hemstitched in bands of six ends. Weave the runner 4⅞in long for a finished length of 4⅝in. Wash the completed piece in mild soap and warm water then iron dry. Trim the fringe to the desired length to finish.

GOTHIC HALLWAY AND LANDING

Within our Gothic villa we put emphasis on the hallway, giving over two major room spaces to create a special feature. Even in the small houses built in row upon row of terraces for the growing middle classes the entrance hall was intended to impress the visitor immediately upon entry. Our walls are painted in picture gallery red and the woodwork, including the stairs, is stained a deep mahogany colour.

This household clearly wants to give an impression of travel, a love of art and perhaps that the householder enjoys the gentlemanly sport of hunting. In evidence are busts and figurines, paintings on the wall and also stored behind the staircase, stuffed animal heads and luggage waiting for removal. The table is actually cast resin, produced by John Hodgson.

The decorative theme continues up the stairs to the landing where there is a small round table covered with a long cloth and topped with a few ornaments – another cream figure, this time a bust, a small dish and a bird in a glass dome. On the wall is one of many samplers that would have adorned the walls of a Victorian house and a stag's head which continues the hunting theme.

Soft furnishings would not have been much in evidence in the hallway as this was a more masculine area, however it does have some rugs and a screen, while the upper landing has a tablecloth and sampler.

This Victorian style hallway has a Gothic Revival feel which was highly popular at the time. The cornice, stair rails, fire surround and flagstone floor were supplied by Sue Cook, while the door and door surrounds were from Angelsey Dolls' Houses and are intended for this house model.

 HALL RUGS

You can make Victorian style rugs that are ideal for a hall or landing by simply selecting pictures from a suitable source and colour photocopying them onto fabric, following the instructions for the photocopied wall hanging in the Elizabethan bedroom, page 21.

TRI-PANEL SCREEN

Screens were an almost indispensable piece of furniture for the Victorians and employed in nearly every room of the house. Their basic function was to keep off draughts but often they were used for privacy or extra decoration. This inexpensive example has been finished with a fabric covering, making it look much more impressive, but you can make a complete screen using the pattern given here. You will need ⅛in thick wood or balsa wood, upholstery fabric, multi-purpose glue, thin ribbon or braid and eight small hinges (optional). You can also use these instructions to cover a bought frame.

First cut three panels from the pattern opposite using ⅛in wood or balsa wood. Alternatively, separate the panels of a bought screen. Using the same pattern cut six pieces of fabric about ⅟₁₆in larger than the pattern all round. Cover one side of each panel by pulling the fabric taut and gluing it along the return edge of the wood. Turn each panel over and cover the other side in exactly the same manner, making sure that no wood shows on the front faces. Trim around all four edges of each panel with thin braid or ribbon to disguise the fabric overlaps. Finally, fix the panels together with the small hinges. Alternatively, arrange the screen so that it will stand and then glue the panels together.

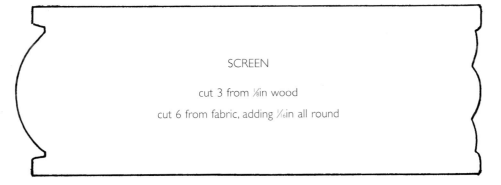

SCREEN

cut 3 from ⅛in wood

cut 6 from fabric, adding ⅛in all round

Fig. 32 Victorian Tri-panel Screen Pattern

UPPER LANDING

Since the hall and landing was regarded as a masculine area there was little need for soft furnishings, but you will find that a few small touches will make all the difference, softening the effect and providing a lived-in look. Our landing features a small occasional table which provides a display surface for a few more of the many ornaments our householder would have. If you do not have space for such a table you might like to provide some other ornamentation such as a rug on the floor as well as a few pictures or samplers on the wall.

TABLECLOTH

Our simple tablecloth on the landing table is made from a woven upholstery fabric with a tiny pattern. To make one you will need your fabric, matching thread, paper for a pattern, a compass, foam core board (polyboard), pins and spray starch.

First measure across the table top then measure the drop from the top to the floor. Double this drop and add it to the first measurement plus an additional 1in for the hem. This will be the diameter of your fabric circle. Set your compass for half the required diameter and use it to draw a circle on paper. This is your pattern. Use it to cut out your fabric, arranging any pattern in the best possible way.

Turn up a ½in hem all round the fabric, easing it into tiny folds on the wrong side, and press with an iron. Stand the table on a piece of foam core board (polyboard) and drape the fabric across the table top – you may wish to protect the table with kitchen film first. Spray the cloth with starch and arrange the table skirt into pleasing folds, pinning the hem to the foam board as you go. When dry remove the pins and kitchen film, if you used it.

ALPHABET, BIRDS AND URN SAMPLER

Adorning the walls of most rooms in the Victorian house, including the stairwell, landings and hall, would have been embroidered samplers. These had been in existence long before the nineteenth century but they were particularly popular at this time. Early samplers were a means by which stitches, patterns, embroidery techniques and skills were taught and recorded and as an added advantage they provided an educational exercise to familiarise young girls with the letters of the alphabet, numbers, bible verses and elements of geography.

This original sampler, by Caren Garfen, is based on designs from the 1830s and features the alphabet and numbers with a decorative design of birds and an urn at the base. It is approximately 1¼ x 2in although the size may differ due to variations in the fabric. To make it you will need 12in square of Kingston cream fabric (approximately 50 hpi), Mulberry silk threads on paper spools in the colours given in the key, a 3½in round embroiderers' flexi-frame and a size 10 needle.

Fit your fabric in the flexi-frame. Each square of the chart represents one stitch. Use one strand of silk thread throughout, working the piece in half cross stitch and following the chart on page 86. Use backstitch to work the outlines marked by a thick black line on the chart. To begin leave approximately 1¼in of thread at the back – this can be sewn in as you progress. Start stitching approximately ¾in from the edge of the flexi-frame, beginning with the zigzag pattern to give a good starting point from which to count stitches for the rest of the design. Once you reach the bird designs, stitch the right-hand bird only with tent stitches going in the opposite direction, i.e. from top left down to bottom right. This gives a better result. There is space in the bottom corners of the sampler to put your own initials (see the photograph, above).

The tablecloth on this table is the main soft furnishing item in this small upper landing, but there is also a hand-stitched tapestry sampler on the wall to make.

Fig. 33 Alphabet, Birds
and Urn Sampler Design

KEY Mulberry silk threads

Green   Z921

Dark gold   Z448

Red   W730

Yellow gold   W7

Lilac   Z158

Green   Z921
(backstitch)

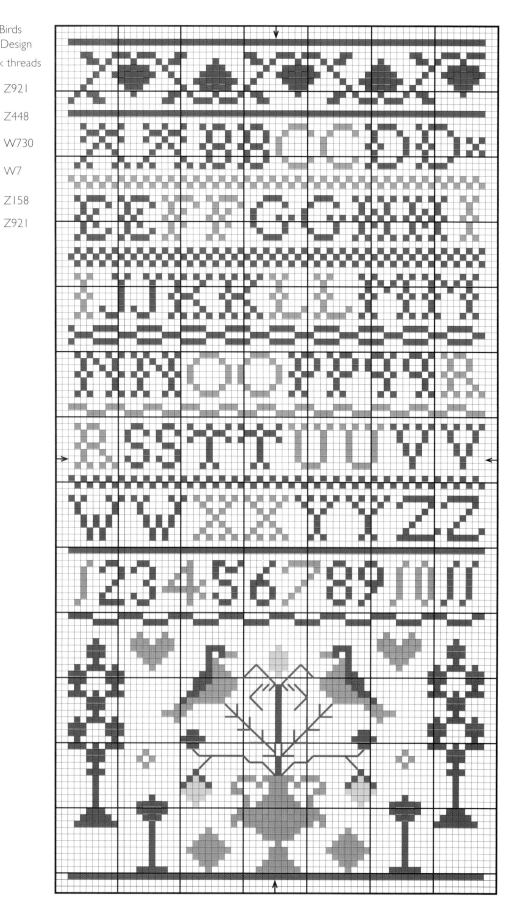

VICTORIAN BEDROOM

A Victorian lady would have had her own private bedroom where she could escape to pursue her favourite pastimes such as reading or embroidery, retire in the afternoon or recover in peace and quiet when she was taken ill. Since it was entirely her own it could be decorated in unashamedly feminine style, with lots of lace, ribbons and flowers. She would have a dressing table which might boast a three panelled mirror, a small hand mirror, brush and comb as well as a few items for her toilet such as face powder. She would need somewhere to house her clothes and she would probably have a large double bed. She might also have a chaise longue so that she could have somewhere to recline during the day. Like all Victorian rooms, there would be many personal touches including samplers and paintings on the walls as well as personal gifts, perhaps brought back by friends and family from abroad.

LACY BEDDING

Now that lace could be made by machine it was more affordable and householders could use it lavishly. They loved it, using it around the house as trims for tablecloths and antimacassars and to cover jars and pillows, for example. In the bedroom there was a host of uses for lace and many a lady's bedroom was lavishly decorated in it. Rosalene Walters, a member of the Miniature Needlework Society, has designed and worked this bedding suitable for

a Victorian style lady's bedroom. The sheet and pillowcases are edged in the same fine crochet work as the bedspread and blanket and are perfect for a very feminine room.

BEDSPREAD

The pretty bedspread which is the crowning piece of the bedding set fits a double bed 4½in wide and 6in long. To make it you will need two 300 metre reels of DMC Broder Machine No 30, a 0.60 crochet hook and rust-proof pins. Work the design following the instructions below.

Abbreviations
ch = chain
st(s) = stitch(es)
beg = beginning
dc = double crochet
tr = treble
htr = half treble
tr 2 tog = half work 2 sts. leaving all loops on the hook, yarn over hook and draw loop through
rep = repeat

Work 134 ch.

Foundation row: 1 tr in 5th ch from hook, 1 tr in next ch, * miss 2 ch, (1 tr, 3 ch, 1 tr) in next ch, miss 2 ch, 1 tr in next 5 ch, rep from * ending with 1 tr in last 3 ch, 3 ch, turn.

1st pattern row: 1 tr in 3rd tr, * 2 ch, 5 tr in 3 ch space, 2 ch, tr 2 tog by working the 1st and 5th sts of 5 tr group tog, rep from * ending by working tr 2 tog in the 2nd last st and the turning ch, 4 ch, turn.

2nd pattern row: 1 tr in 1st tr, * 1 tr in next 5 tr, (1 tr, 3 ch, 1 tr) in the centre of tr 2 tog, rep from * ending with (1 tr, 1 ch, 1 tr) in turning ch, 3 ch, turn.

3rd pattern row: 2 tr in 1 ch, space, * 2 ch, tr 2 tog by working the 1st and 5th sts of 5 tr group tog, 2 ch, 5 tr in 3 ch space, rep from * ending with 3 tr in turning ch, 3 ch, turn.

4th pattern row: Miss 1st st, 1 tr in next 2 tr, * (1 tr, 3 ch, 1 tr) in the centre of tr 2 tog, 1 tr in next 5 tr, rep from * ending with 1 tr in last 2 tr, 1 tr in turning ch, 3 ch, turn.

Repeat the four pattern rows 11 times more or to the length required. Fasten off.

FOR THE EDGING work 6 ch.

Foundation row: Work (1 tr, 2 ch, 1 tr, 2 ch, 1 tr) in the 6th ch from hook, 5 ch, turn.

Pattern row: Work (1 tr, 2 ch, 1 tr, 2 ch, 1 tr) in the centre tr of the previous row, 5 ch, turn.

Repeat the pattern row for approximately 20in or until the edging fits around the two sides and bottom edges, allowing for a slight gathering at the bottom corners. Do not turn.

Heading: * 1 dc in next 5 ch loop, 6 ch, rep from * ending with 3 ch, 1 dc into last ch on the foundation row. Fasten off. Using the same cotton attach the edging to the bedspread with slipstitch. Dampen the bedspread. Using rust-proof pins, pin out to shape. Press using a medium hot iron.

LACE-TRIMMED SHEETS

The top sheet is trimmed with the same edging as the bedspread for a co-ordinated look. First, simply make the bed sheets from fine cotton material in the same way as the sheets in the Elizabethan bedroom (see page 15). Then make enough edging to trim the top edge of the top sheet following the instructions given for the bedspread and attach to the sheet with slipstitch.

LACE-TRIMMED PILLOWS

To make these lovely matching pillows you will need fine cotton fabric, the crochet materials used for the bedspread and some polyester stuffing.

For each pillow cut two pieces of fine cotton approximately 2¾ x 2¼in. Pin them together with raw edges matching and sew a ¼in seam around three edges using backstitch. Turn to the right side and stuff lightly with polyester stuffing then tuck in the ¼in seam allowances along the open edge and slipstitch the gap closed. Make approximately 20in of the bedspread edging to go all the way around the pillow, allowing for a certain amount of gathering, then slipstitch in place to finish.

CROCHETED BLANKET

Crocheted blankets were popular in Victorian times, sometimes worked in brightly coloured sections or sometimes as one piece. This one is made in a creamy white colour but you could choose any colour that suits your room scheme. To make it you will need four 50 metre balls of 1 ply yarn, a 1.00 crochet hook and 8in of 5/8in wide satin ribbon for a trim. For an explanation of the abbreviations see left.

Work 85 ch.

1 dc in 2nd ch from hook, 1 dc in each ch to end, 2 ch, turn. (84 dc + turning ch).

1st pattern row: Miss 1st st, 1 htr in next and every dc to end, 1 htr in turning ch, 1 ch, turn.

2nd pattern row: Miss 1st st, 1 dc in next and every htr to end, 1 dc in turning ch, 2 ch, turn.

Repeat the 1st and 2nd pattern rows until work measures approximately 7in or is the length required.

Work a row of dc all round working 3 dc at each corner. Fasten off. Sew in all ends.

Fold the ribbon in half and sew to the top of the blanket as a trim.

ARTS & CRAFTS PARLOUR

This miniature room was actually based on a real-life design illustrated in the *British Architect* of 1884. Supported by William Morris, the scheme was aimed at artisans to guide them in the furnishing of their cottage homes in order to improve their lives. Unfortunately the idea failed as furniture and furnishing produced in the Arts & Crafts ideal proved too expensive for any but the richest followers. Nevertheless, the style did enjoy some popularity with the more well-to-do who rejected the conformity of mass produced goods and regimented housing.

Here the work of William Morris is represented by the wallpaper in a Tom Tit design, the screen and cushions in Morris's Celandine design, the central rug and sampler and in the ladder back chairs. The room has a deep-set window on one side permitting the inclusion of an upholstered window seat. The floor, skirting board, dado rail and much of the furniture is stained natural wood but the top section of the walls and the heavily beamed ceiling are all painted a creamy white. In keeping with the style and period, decorative objects displayed are intended to be both attractive and useful and ideally made by hand. The fern and bamboo picture frames are borrowed from other Victorian popular ideas but illustrate how a room should reflect the taste of the imaginary inhabitant.

Soft furnishings within the room are the upholstered wing chair, the curtains, window seat cushion, sampler, tapestry carpet, fireside rug, screen, lamp shade, squab cushions, table mats and footstool.

✂ UPHOLSTERED WING CHAIR

Once you get the hang of it re-upholstering inexpensive imported furniture with your own special fabric can be most rewarding. The basic wing chair used here is readily available. With only minor alterations it has been customised for the part. You will need the chair, suitable fabric and multi-purpose glue.

Start by removing all the outer layers of covered card, the seat cushion, arm, wings and finally the back. Keep a note of the order in which you removed the pieces so you can reassemble the cover easily. If possible, unpeel the fabric from the forms and reuse them as patterns for cutting your own fabric. To alter this chair to suit the room

better we removed the top curve of the back parts from both the forms and the fabric pattern.

Cut new fabric pieces using the forms or old fabric pieces as a guide, making sure the fabric is about ⅛in larger all round than the forms. Lay out each fabric piece, wrong side up, and centre the corresponding form on top. Fold the excess fabric over the card around the edges and glue in place, paying special attention to corners to ensure a neat finish and trimming off the excess fabric here as necessary. When the glue has dried reassemble the piece in reverse order using a strong glue. As a final touch we also changed the legs of this chair to give it a more Victorian feel.

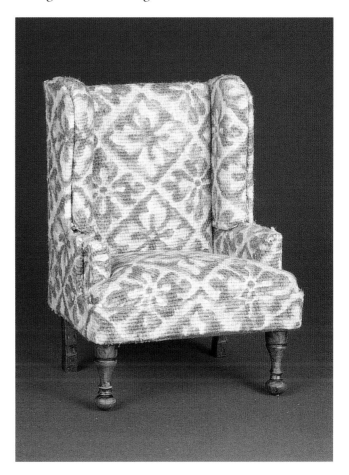

✂ SHORT CURTAINS

As these curtains were required to fit inside a window frame, calculating the right length was crucial. Take a measurement from the top of the curtain pole to the seat or floor and measure the width of the whole window. Add an extra 1in to the length. Cut two curtains this size, then follow the instructions for the velvet curtain in the Stuart drawing room to make them (see page 28).

This cottage parlour of 1884 is very much influenced by the Arts & Crafts Movement. Accessories include the flowers by Gill Rawling of Petite Fleur and the William Morris style chairs by Kim Selwood. The figure is by doll artist James Carrington.

X WINDOW SEAT CUSHION

The window seat cushion is made from the same fabric as the curtains and makes this a snug place to sit. You will need suitable fabric, thick card or modelling board, a padding of foam, wadding or tissue and multi-purpose glue.

First make a paper pattern of the top of the window seat and check the fit. When you are satisfied with your pattern cut it from thick card or modelling board. Cover the card with your padding of foam, wadding or tissue which has been cut to fit. Now cut your fabric from the pattern, adding at least ¼in extra all round. Lay the fabric over the seat pad and glue the turnings to the underside, making sure that the front edge of the cushion is neat as this is the only one to show. Fit the cushion on the window seat.

SQUAB CUSHIONS

A selection of squab cushions provide the finishing touch on the window seat. Their fabric was produced in a rather clever way by photocopying a William Morris design of 1896 known as Celandine or Harebell onto plain fabric. The pattern of the design can be reduced to the correct scale at the same time (see photocopied wall hanging, page 21). You will need fabric, matching thread and a stuffing such as rice, salt or cotton wool.

To make the cushions first make a paper pattern 2in square and pin it onto your photocopied fabric, making sure the design is centred. Use sharp scissors to cut two fabric squares for each cushion. We used the same fabric for the front and back but a plain colour can be used for the reverse side, if preferred. Pin the squares together with right sides facing and stitch around three sides, taking an ⅛in seam allowance. Turn the cushion out and fill with your choice of filling: rice or salt produce a pliable cushion but cotton wool or similar may also be used, if preferred. Tuck in the seam allowances on the open edge and slipstitch closed.

X TABLE MAT

A simple little table mat made from an evenweave fine cotton fabric was fashioned to cover the side table. This type of mat is easy to make by cutting the fabric to shape and then fraying the edges. To do this just pull out the cross threads with a pin until the fringe is the desired length. Then fuse iron-on interfacing onto the back of the fabric to prevent further fraying, if desired. Our table mat fabric was 1¾ x 1⅛in and then the edges were frayed to about ⅜in, but you can make the mat whatever size you like.

X LAMP SHADE

This lamp shade is simply a fringe hanging from a brass ring and it looks very appropriate in this room. It is easy to make from a metal ring and a piece of white silk fabric. You will also need multi-purpose glue and a fine brass pin.

To make the lamp shade take a 2½ x 2in piece of fine white silk fabric and press if necessary. Place the silk on a clean, flat surface. Find the centre of the 2in edge by folding the fabric in half, then use a fine brass pin to pull out single vertical threads from left and right of the centre to a depth of 1in, leaving ½in at each end. Fold the fabric in half and neatly glue it around the inside of a ring or disc. (It may be necessary to trim the length to fit.) The finished length of the shade when folded should be 1in. The pulled-thread section when folded should be ½in long.

X ARTS & CRAFTS SCREEN

The Victorians' love of screens even managed to continue on into the Arts & Crafts style towards the end of the era. Our screen has been made by cannibalising two model kits for dinner gongs. (The actual gong of one has been turned into the light fitting in the room.) New centre panels have been made and covered in the same way as the seat cushion (see above). Alternatively, you can cut your own screen from wood as we did in the Victorian hall (see page 82) or buy a ready made screen or screen kit.

FOOT STOOL

Our figure is resting her feet comfortably on a velvet footstool which is easily made from paper or thin card, fabric, matching Pearsall's silk gossamer thread, sewing thread and foam. This one was constructed using a patchwork technique by wrapping the fabric around card and then oversewing the pieces together.

To make a footstool like this first decide on the size. This one was 1½ x 1 x ¾in. Cut two patterns from paper or thin card for the long sides (1½ x ¾in), two for the ends (1 x ¾in) and one each for the top and base (1½ x 1in). Place each pattern on your fabric and cut out, allowing ¼in extra around each edge. Fold the fabric pieces over your paper/card templates, press and then tack (baste) the fabric onto the paper/card. Use silk gossamer thread to

oversew the fabric pieces together, leaving one end open to fill. Fill with a small block of foam and close the gap by oversewing. Carefully remove the tacking (basting) threads, leaving the paper or card shapes in place.

TATTED TABLE MATS

Tatting is a form of fancy work which is sometimes used as a preliminary training for crochet. It is composed of knots or stitches and loops or picots which are drawn up into circles or semi-circles to produce looped or swirling lace patterns and it is worked by wrapping the thread around your fingers and then passing a shuttle of thread over and under that thread. The technique was at its greatest popularity in the eighteenth century but still would have been favoured in Victorian times to make, for example, an edging for a handkerchief. Since it is possible to create very fine work with tatting it is ideal for miniature settings. Here it is used to make two table mats. You will need some tatting experience to make them,

but it is not a difficult craft to learn, particularly if you can already knit or crochet.

FOUR CROSSES TABLE RUNNER

This table runner was designed by Lynne Johnson. Work the table runner following the instructions opposite, making sure all tying and sewing of threads is done on the same side. You will need fine tatting cotton, a shuttle, tatting hook and spray starch. When winding the shuttle allow three winds of a standard shuttle for each ring of similar size to the design illustrated. This should be plenty and should help avoid having to join threads halfway round a row. Try to sew the ends round a ring where possible for a neat finish and keep the picots small and even unless the pattern is enhanced by graduating to larger then smaller. When joining chain row to chain row the effect is more pleasing if the picot that will be used for joining is small. 'Tweak' the picots when finished (at least those that show the most).

Work a ring of 6ds, p, 6ds. Close ring. Reverse work.

Chain of 2ds, 5p sep 2ds, 2ds. Reverse work.

Ring of 6ds, join to p on prev ring, 6ds. Close ring.

Close to last ring work a 2nd ring of 6ds, p, 6ds. Close ring. Reverse work.

Chain of 2ds, 5p sep 2ds, 2ds. Reverse work.

Ring of 6ds, j to p of prev ring, 6ds. Close ring.

Close to last ring work a 2nd ring of 6ds, p, 6ds. Close ring. Reverse work.

Continue until 10 chains have been worked. Reverse work.

Work ring as before, 6ds, join to p of prev ring, 6ds. Close ring.

Close to last ring work a 2nd ring of 6ds, p, 6ds. Close ring. Reverse work.

Chain of 2ds, 5p sep 2ds, 2ds. Reverse work.

Ring of 6ds, join to p of prev ring, 6ds. Close ring. Reverse work.

To turn corner Chain of 2ds, 5p sep 2ds, 2ds. Reverse work.

Ring of 6ds, join to p of paired rings above, 6ds. Close ring. Reverse work.

Chain of 2ds, 5p sep 2ds, 2ds. Reverse work.

Ring of 6ds, j to p of 3 joined rings above, 6ds. Close ring. (This makes a cross of four rings joining at the centre). Close to last ring work a 2nd ring of 6ds, j to p of next paired rings above, close ring. Reverse work.

Chain of 2ds, 5p sep 2ds, 2ds. Reverse work.

Abbreviations
d = double stitch
p = picot
sep = separate
prev = previous
j = join

Continue until 11 crosses of four rings joining at the centre have been formed. Reverse work after last ring.

Chain of 2ds, 5p sep 2ds, 2ds. Join to base of 1st ring. Cut, tie the threads and sew in the ends.

Work a 2nd strip the same but joining the centre p of each chain on the top side of 2nd strip to the centre p of every chain on the bottom side of 1st strip.

To work a cross of four rings at each end Ring of 6ds, p, 6ds. Close ring. Reverse work.

Chain of 2ds, 5p sep 2ds, 2ds. Reverse work.

Ring of 6ds, join to p of prev ring, 6ds. Close ring. Reverse work.

Chain of 2ds, 4p sep 2ds, join to 4th p (from left) of end chain on left strip, 2ds. Reverse work.

Ring of 6ds, join to p of prev paired rings, 6ds. Close ring. Reverse work.

Chain of 2ds, p, 2ds, join to 1st p of left-hand chain that joins strips together, 2ds, p, 2ds, join to last p of right-hand chain that joins strips together, 2ds, p, 2ds. Reverse work.

Ring of 6ds, join to p of 3 joining rings (making a cross of four), 6ds. Close ring. Reverse work.

Chain of 2ds, join to 2nd p of end chain of right strip, 2ds, 4p sep 2ds, 2ds. Join to base of first ring. Cut and tie the thread and sew in the ends.

Repeat the cross of four rings at the other end in exactly the same way.

Press the finished mat using spray starch for a crisp finish.

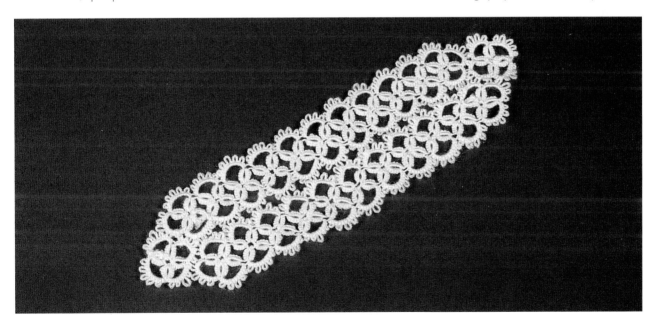

The tatted table runner has been enlarged so that you can see the detail in it more easily. Use this photograph as an aid when following the instructions above.

 TREFOIL TABLE MAT

This pretty table mat is quick to make using fine cotton tatting thread, a shuttle, tatting hook and spray starch. For best results refer to the general tatting instructions given at the start of the Four Crosses Table Runner where you will also find an explanation of the abbreviations. You will need basic tatting experience to make this mat.

With the shuttle thread make a ring of 3ds, 5p sep 3ds, 3ds. Close ring.

Close to first ring work a second ring of 3ds, j to last p of prev ring, 3ds, 6p sep 3ds, 3ds. Close ring.

Close to last ring work a third ring of 3ds, j to last p of last ring, 3ds, 4p sep 3ds, 3ds. Close ring. Reverse work.

Chain of 3ds, 8p sep 3ds, 3ds. Reverse work.

Repeat another set of three rings, joining 3rd p of 1st ring to 2nd free p of last ring of prev set of rings.

Reverse work.

Chain of 3ds, j to last p of prev chain, 3ds, 7p sep 3ds, 3ds. Reverse work.

Continue this pattern until seven sets of three rings have been completed.

Chain of 3ds, j to last p of prev chain, 3ds, 2p sep 3ds, 3ds. Reverse work.

Set of three rings, joining 2nd and 3rd p of 1st ring to 2nd and 3rd free p of last ring of prev set of rings. Reverse work.

Chain of 3ds, j to last p of prev short chain, 3ds, 2p sep 3ds, 3ds. Reverse work.

Set of three rings, joining as last set. Reverse work.

Chain of 3ds, j to last p of prev short chain, 3ds, 2p sep 3ds, 3ds, join next two p to middle two p of parallel chain (last long chain worked), 3ds, 3p sep 3ds, 3ds. Reverse work.

Set of three rings joining 3rd p of 1st ring to 2nd free p of last ring of prev set of rings. Reverse work.

Chain, as before, joining 1st p to last p of prev long chain and joining middle two ps to middle two ps of parallel chain.

Continue all round until seven sets of three rings have been worked on each side with one set of three rings at each end, joined by short chains. Finish off and press the finished mat using spray starch for a crisp finish.

 FIRESIDE RUG

A small rug in front of the fire would add to the cosy feeling of the room. You can make one very simply by photocopying a picture of a suitable rug onto fabric – just follow the instructions for the photocopied wall hanging in the Elizabethan bedroom (see page 21). Another alternative to the tapestry rug below is to make a rug from fabric (see the simple drugget in the Regency dining room on page 61).

WILLIAM MORRIS CARPET

This design by Sue Bakker has been adapted from a small hand-knotted pile carpet of the late nineteenth century designed by William Morris and made at the Hammersmith workshop. The miniature carpet in this room was hand worked, following the pattern, by keen miniaturist John Roebuck who kindly loaned it for the setting. It measures 9¼ x 5½in on 18-count canvas, 7½ x 4½in

Fig. 34 William Morris Carpet Design

KEY DMC stranded cotton

Light peach 543
Mid peach 758
Blue 926
Light blue 927
Green 3052
Dark peach 3778
Ecru
Red 347+355
Dark blue 930+3750

on 22-count canvas and 5½ x 3⅜in on 30-count canvas. To make it you will need canvas or gauze in one of the sizes specified, a tapestry needle (No. 24 for 18 and 22-count canvas and No. 26 for 30-count gauze), an embroidery frame, and DMC stranded embroidery cottons in the colours listed in the key on page 97.

Use two strands of cotton throughout, working the piece in half cross stitch and the background areas in basketweave stitch (see page 158). Following the chart on page 97, begin in the centre and work outwards. Work the central background area in dark blue (930 and 3750) and the border background in red (347 and 355). Start working with a 'waste' knot and end by threading the needle through the backs of previous stitches. For more advice on working from a quarter pattern, see page 36.

⊠ ALPHABET SAMPLER

Annelle Fergusson, a fellow of IGMA, designed this Victorian Alphabet Sampler for our parlour. It measure 1⅜in wide and 1⅞in high with a stitch count of 65 across the width and 77 in height. To make it you will need 48-count silk gauze, a size 10 crewel needle and DMC stranded embroidery cottons in the colours listed in the key. You will also need cardboard and masking tape plus a frame for mounting the finished design.

Mount the gauze in a cardboard frame with a window cut in it slightly larger than the design (see page

156). Use one strand of cotton throughout to work the design in half cross stitch, changing to basketweave stitch to work background areas because this causes less distortion of the gauze (see page 158). Start at the centre and work to the edges, filling the border around the alphabet in gold. When you work the background allow a five stitch border from the edge of the worked pattern. For more advice, refer to Using a Chart, page 157.

Remove the finished work from the card frame and steam iron it with the wrong side up, using a pressing cloth to protect the stitches. Leave the sampler to dry for 24 hours before framing.

Fig. 35 Victorian Alphabet Sampler Design
KEY DMC stranded cotton

■	Red	356	■	Gold	729	■	Light blue	927
■	Light gold	676	■	Mid blue	926	■	Green	3053

■ Dark blue 924 (background)

This stylish Edwardian nursery is furnished with a bed, washstand, towel rail, bedside cabinet and work box all from Edwardian Elegance. The pretty washstand set with matching potty were made by Stokesay Ware.

EARLY 20TH CENTURY STYLE

By the turn of the century a new found freedom for women, a shortage of domestic servants and the introduction of family planning dictated that the home of the early 1900s should be smaller and easier to manage. The new century brought with it a whole host of new inventions many of which could now be put to use within the home. Slowly but surely a fondness for over-decoration and a love of fancy ornaments gave way to interiors that were simpler and brighter and which could be run more easily. Fewer fabrics were used with heavy brocades and velvets giving way to lightweight printed cottons and later synthetic fabrics. Hygiene was a key word and unnecessary draperies, particularly in nurseries and bedrooms, were very much frowned upon. In new homes indoor lavatories and bathrooms were considered a necessity and the development of linoleum was particularly advantageous for these. Overall houses were now smaller, even for the middle classes, and usually built on just two stories. Designers such as Edwin Lutyens, Charles Voysey and to a lesser degree Charles Rennie Mackintosh and in America Frank Lloyd Wright were greatly influential. All advocated the use of white and pale colours for home interior decoration.

❋　　❋　　❋

At this time fitted furniture was becoming the order of the day, with built in cupboards, inglenooks and seats in niches which gave rooms a more spacious feel. More delicate, paler coloured furniture helped complete the look. Wallpapers were now in pale colours and with the exception of the hall the dado rail disappeared, often to be replaced by a top frieze or low border at skirting-board level. Woodwork was usually painted off-white including doors which sometimes had a painted stencil design of Art Nouveau motif upon them.

The style of Art Nouveau to some extent grew from the Arts & Crafts movement and achieved a certain popularity from the 1890s and into the early 1900s. It took its inspiration from flowing plant forms, both stylised and sinuous, which adapted well to the requirement for less heavy furniture. Motifs of flowers and plants, particularly roses, appeared in the form of lamps, vases, furniture and all manner of plaster and metal work and as printed decorations on tiles, wallpaper and fabrics. The favoured colours were predominantly pinks, mauves, greens, blues and turquoises. After the Paris Exposition *Des Arts Decoratifs* in 1925 the more dramatic styling of Art Deco took over from Art Nouveau. Forms were geometric and colours bold with furniture and furnishings constructed either from new materials or new manufacturing techniques.

After the outbreak of the Second World War for most of Europe at least thoughts of home and interior design were more or less put on hold. The only 1940s styling seen came by way of the cinema and America's Hollywood movies.

The long climb back from the austerity of the war years meant that homes, although brighter and more airy, were of necessity perhaps a little frugal with decoration. Touches of colour were usually added to the home with accessories. Bright red, sky blue, rich yellow and clever use of black, white or even grey would appear as chair seats, cushions, a vase or clock, or printed pattern on curtains and carpets.

EDWARDIAN NURSERY

Traditionally in Victorian and Edwardian homes nurseries, lesser bedrooms and servants' quarters would be furnished with items no longer required in more important areas of the house. Not so this nursery, for it has furniture in typical period styling. The walls are in an up to date pale paper and are topped with a lovely children's frieze of Kate Greenaway design while paintwork and ceiling are finished in off-white.

Bedding is clear of the wooden floor on both the cot and Nanny's bed for easy sweeping and the room is illuminated by a modern electric light bulb.

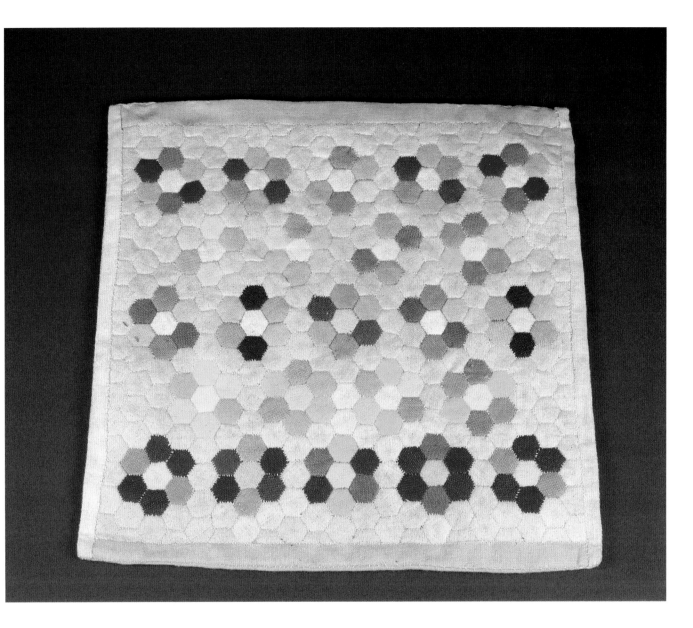

In the room the soft furnishings are few as it was considered more hygienic at the time to limit the use of fabrics. They include the cot bedding, Nanny's bed with patchwork quilt, towels, a rag rug and sampler.

NANNY'S BED

This practical but comfortable looking bed has been kitted out with some soft bedding to make Nanny as cosy as possible. In particular it has a beautiful flower garden quilt in cream, pinks and yellows which was made in the same way as a full-size quilt. To make the mattresses, sheets and pillow refer to the instructions for the Elizabethan bed starting on page 14. Note that since this is a single bed you will need to make all the items smaller

to fit. Alternatively, refer to the instructions for the Shaker bed on page 150 which is also a single.

 FLOWER GARDEN QUILT

This quilt, created by Fiona Bailey, has a traditional pattern created from hexagons stitched together to make flowers. The flowers, usually in a patterned fabric, are linked by a plain 'path' of hexagons. Here plain, autumnal shades have been used for the flowers with a light beige colour for the paths. The quilt is backed with a plain piece of cotton lawn and borders are made with strips of fabric. To make the quilt you will need cotton fabric for the hexagons, cotton lawn or silk fabric for lining, Lills pins, a No. 11 needle, silk gossamer thread, tacking thread, scissors, paper and thin card.

The quilt shown is 6in square. To make it you will need approximately 380 hexagons – seven individual hexagons for each flower and additional hexagons for the paths. Start by making a hexagonal pattern. To do this lay out a piece of thin card or plastic. Use a compass and draw a circle with a radius the same distance as one of the sides of the required hexagon, in this case ⁵⁄₁₆in. Then, keeping the compass radius set, place the point of the compass at any point on the circle and mark along the circumference. Move the point to the mark and continue marking along the circumference until you have made six marks. Draw straight lines to connect the marks to create a perfect hexagonal shape.

Use the template to cut 380 paper hexagons. Cut the same number of fabric hexagons, adding small seam allowances all round – for this quilt you will need 23 flower centres, 138 petals and 119 paths. Next cover each paper shape by folding a fabric hexagon around it, ensuring that the angles remain true. Carefully tack the fabric onto the paper hexagon. This can be tricky. As you work the pressure from your fingers will press the fabric into shape.

Make a flower by joining six hexagons around a central hexagon using whipstitch and working with right sides facing. Make 23 flowers – more for a larger quilt. Join the path pieces to the flowers using the photograph on page 103 as a guide. The path hexagons will need to be trimmed to ensure a flat edge. When you have joined all the hexagons together carefully remove the paper hexagons from the fabric and press with an iron.

Cut backing fabric the same size as the quilt front and lay it out. Pin the quilt on top with right sides out. Cut narrow strips of fabric to make a border for all four sides of the quilt and then stitch them to the quilt and backing like binding (see page 161). Alternatively, cut the backing fabric larger than the quilt and wrap the excess over to the front on all edges, turning in the raw ends to form the border.

⊞ BIBLE SAMPLER

Religious sayings were popular for samplers throughout the ages, and would have been placed in the nursery to inspire the child and perhaps also to offer a certain degree of protection. This one may have been worked by a member of an earlier generation and passed down through the family. It is designed by Caren Garfen and measures approximately 1 x ¾in, although the size will vary slightly depending on your fabric. Since it is so tiny it is useful to have a magnifying glass to help you see what you are doing. Those with a lamp attached are particularly handy.

To make the sampler you will need a 10in square of Kingston cream fabric (approximately 50 hpi), Mulberry silk threads on paper spools in the colours given in the key opposite, a 3½in round flexi-frame, a size 10 needle and small, sharp scissors.

Each square of the chart represents one tent stitch (half cross stitch) worked with one strand of silk thread. Each stitch crosses over one thread in each direction of the fabric. Where a thick black line is printed on the chart work the line in backstitch. To hold your work while you stitch, fit the fabric in the flexi-frame. Following the chart opposite, begin at the top left-hand corner and work the design from top to bottom, starting approximately ¾in from the edge of the flexi-frame. To begin leave approximately 1in of thread at the back – this can be sewn in as you progress. Stitch the border first, commencing with mid green; this gives a good starting point from which to count stitches for the rest of the design. For more advice refer to Using a Chart, page 157.

Fig. 36 Bible Sampler Design
KEY Mulberry silk threads

| ● | Light green | W255 | ▼ | Burnt orange | Z377 |
| ■ | Mid green | W561 | ◇ | Dark brown | Z776 |

TOWELS

The towels featured in this room were made from a piece of old, finely woven pure-cotton fabric with a slight texture. This makes the towels look a little coarse rather than soft and fluffy, suggesting that they are not the best towels in the house.

To make the towels cut your fabric to fit the towel rails – ours were 1⅜ x 3in. Finish all four sides with tiny blanket stitch using cotton thread.

STRIPED COT QUILT

The striped cot quilt (shown at right) was designed by Sheila Grantham and is made using a technique popular around 1880-1890 when patchwork blocks were made from overlapping strips of folded fabric. For this miniature version the blocks are made using fine silk ribbon.

To make the quilt you will need five 5 x 2in pieces of fine cotton lawn or muslin, 20in of ⅜in wide fine silk ribbon in each of eight colours, a 3¼in square of fine plain silk to match the ribbons for backing, a 2¾in square of fine cotton lawn for interlining and fine silk sewing threads (to tone or contrast).

Trace the block strip template given below onto each of your cotton lawn or muslin strips. Mark on both sides of the fabric because you will lay the silk ribbon on one side and sew and cut from the other side. Cut the silk ribbon into 3¾in lengths and position five strips horizontally over the first strip of lawn or muslin so that

This colourful cot quilt is made from silk ribbon strips sewn together and then cut into blocks, so it is quicker to make than you might think. Its finished size should be 3½ x 3½ in.

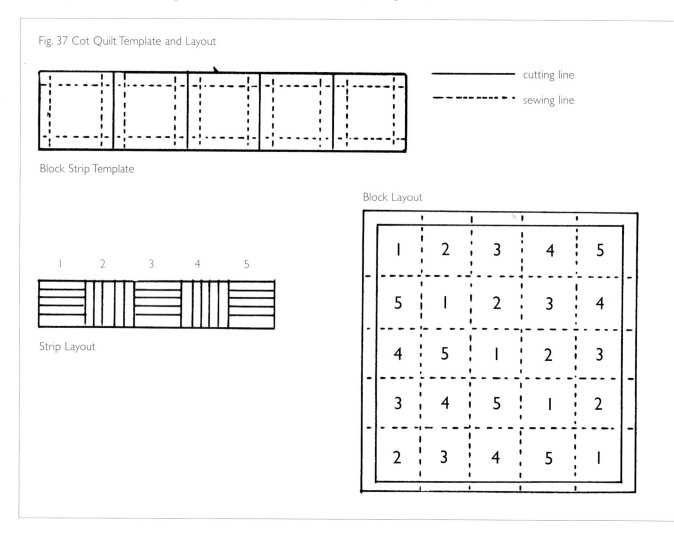

Fig. 37 Cot Quilt Template and Layout

——————— cutting line

– – – – – – – sewing line

Block Strip Template

Strip Layout

1 2 3 4 5

Block Layout

1	2	3	4	5
5	1	2	3	4
4	5	1	2	3
3	4	5	1	2
2	3	4	5	1

they overlap. Sew them down on the overlap with a small running stitch. Cut the strip into five blocks, carefully following the cutting lines marked on the back. Repeat to cover the other four strips with ribbon using different colours and arrangements of silk ribbon and then cut into individual blocks. You should now have a total of 25 blocks.

Take one block from each group and join into a strip as shown in the strip layout. Press open each seam. Make up another four strips in the same way but stagger the block designs as shown in the block layout. Now join the strips together to make a large square. To assemble the quilt lay out the lining, right side down. Centre the interlining on top and then the quilt front, right side up. Tack the layers together. With the quilt side facing up

fold, tack and press down a border of ⅛in of the backing silk on all sides. Fold over an ⅛in again and slipstitch neatly to the quilt front. Remove your tacking stitches and lightly press the finished quilt.

RAG RUG

A small rug such as this helps to provide a little bit of comfort in an otherwise minimally decorated room. This one is woven in colours which link in with the autumnal colours used for Nanny's quilt. In fact, you could use your left over fabric to make it. Our rug was woven by Ina Wichers. To make it simply follow the instructions for the rag rug in the Larsson style room (see pages 145 and 146).

If you don't have a loom to weave this rag rug, simply make it from plaited fabric strips (see page 143). Make it whatever size seems suitable for the setting.

1930s Living Room

The beginning of the 1930s saw the growth of town suburbs as building developers engulfed the landscape with countless interpretations of mock Tudor dwellings. New homes meant new lives away from the old city centres. Naturally, not everyone moved from their existing home and many larger houses were modernised. Here we have decorated the drawing room of our Gothic Villa as it may have looked in the 1930s. It is unlikely that any structural changes would have been made, so the ceiling rose and cornice of the original house remain. However, the fireplace has been changed for one finished in red brick. This style was popular at the time as somehow it reflected the ideals of traditional hearth and home.

The ceiling light fitting is now electric as are the two wall lights in mock-Tudor styling located above the fireplace. The dado rail has gone and the wallpaper is fairly pale, having a small design in just one toning colour. Curtains are simple and hang straight with their pole and fixings disguised behind a pelmet. Furniture items are representative of those available at the time but together create a cosy look rather than one that is stylish. The chest and open court cupboard are of mock-Jacobean taste whilst the armchairs and low table are much more Art Deco. Other details typical of the period are the carpet, leather pouf, standard lamp, Clarice Cliff style vases, flying ducks on the wall and the antimacassars on the backs of the armchairs.

Soft furnishings in this room comprise the armchair, leather pouf, chair cover, curtains, lamp shade, woven tablecloth, carpet and the crocheted antimacassar, mats and runner.

This 1930s living room features two comfortable arm-chairs and a leather pouf which are easily made from fabric-covered wood or balsa.

X 1930s ARMCHAIR

The design for this ½ scale armchair has been taken directly from an old idea of making dolls' house furniture from match boxes. Although simple to make it looks very effective, particularly when topped with a crocheted antimacassar (see page 115). To make it you will need ½in wood, balsa or foam core, suitable fabric, thin card, a padding of foam, wadding or cotton wool and some multi-purpose glue. Use a fabric with a tiny pattern or choose fake leather or suede for an authentic look.

From ½in wood, balsa or foam core cut two blocks from pattern A for the arms and three blocks from pattern B for the chair base, seat cushion and back. From suitable fabric cut two pieces from pattern C to cover the arms and three from pattern D for the base, cushion cover and back. Then cut six pieces of thin card from pattern E. Finally, cut six fabric pieces from pattern F.

Cover the wood arms (A) with fabric, making sure the two sides correspond to the broken line on the pattern. Glue the fabric in place at the ends. Cover the seat base (B) in the same way. Place a small piece of foam,

Fig. 38 1930s Armchair Patterns

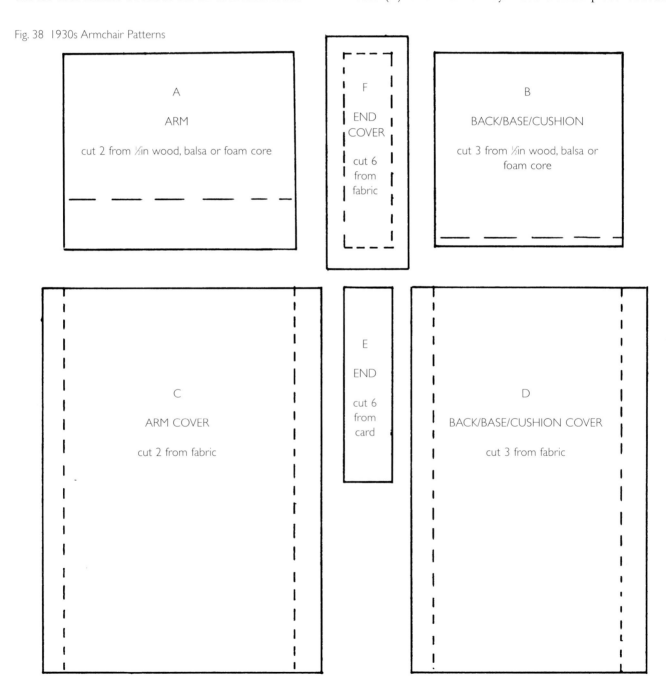

A

ARM

cut 2 from ½in wood, balsa or foam core

F

END COVER

cut 6 from fabric

B

BACK/BASE/CUSHION

cut 3 from ½in wood, balsa or foam core

C

ARM COVER

cut 2 from fabric

E

END

cut 6 from card

D

BACK/BASE/CUSHION COVER

cut 3 from fabric

wadding or cotton wool on one side of the chair back (B) and on the top of the seat cushion (B), then cover these two blocks in the same way as the chair base. Cover the six pieces of thin card with their material, turning the fabric edges over and gluing them on the back of the card. When the glue is dry, stick the four pieces of covered card to the front and back ends of the arms and two pieces to the ends of the back. Assemble the chair by gluing the seat cushion to the base and the arms to the sides of the cushion and base, then add the back at a slight angle.

For a different look the arms could be covered in an alternative fabric from the back or seat cushion or the front of the arms could be trimmed with fine braid in a contrasting colour.

 ## LEATHER POUF

Leather poufs were very much part of the 1930s look, so we simply had to make one for this room setting. This one is made in a warm brown colour which complements the armchairs beautifully. It is based on a piece of wooden dowel or a plastic cap from an aerosol can about 1¼in in diameter and covered with real leather. To make

it you will also need some multi-purpose glue, thin card, and an optional trim of cord or embroidery cotton.

Cut a piece of soft leather the circumference of the dowel base (or plastic cap) by its height plus about ½in. Cover the dowel by gluing the leather onto it, forming a butt joint on the side and turning over the excess material at top and bottom. Next cut a disc of thin card to the same diameter as the dowel or cap and cut a piece of leather slightly larger all round. Glue this to the card disc, turning the extra leather over to the back. Glue the leather-covered disc to the top of the dowel or cap and trim around the join and base if required with fine cord or embroidery cotton, as shown above.

 ## CHAIR COVER

Just visible at the back of this living room is a dining chair made from a plastic kit. The seat for this chair can be covered with fabric. First remove the plastic seat piece and cut a piece of fabric slightly larger all round. Snap the fabric and the seat into position from underneath the chair, pulling the fabric smoothly in place as you do so and then trim away any excess fabric.

MINIATURE PILE CARPET

The carpet in this room was designed and woven by Clare Minty on a 24-shaft dobby loom. As the carpet is a 14 block pattern it actually uses only 16 of these shafts. However, as each pattern block requires four different sheds, a total of 56 treadles would be needed to weave the piece. This makes the use of a dobby loom the only reasonably practical way of weaving this type of carpet. To make it possible for more people to attempt to weave their own carpet we have given the weaving draft for a two-block carpet which can be woven on any loom with four shafts and eight treadles. Use sewing thread for the warp and fine chenille for the weft.

Start by designing a two-block profile draft or use the one provided right. Then write out the threading and treadling draft in the usual way or use the one included. Substitute the threading for Block A where

you have a Block A in your profile and threading Block B where Block B appears in the profile. You may repeat threading Blocks A and B to build up your pattern.

Using a strong sewing thread as warp yarn, make a warp with its length equal to the number of carpets you want to weave multiplied by the length of the carpets (there is hardly any take up in the length) plus the expected loom wastage. The width of the warp will be the width of the carpet plus +/- 8% draw (depending on your weaving style and the yarns that you use for weft) multiplied by the number of ends per inch. Warp the loom in your usual way, making sure that the warp goes on tightly and evenly. Sley in a metric 40/10 reed or equivalent at 30 ends per inch (12 ends per cm) and 3 ends per dent. Tie on tightly and evenly. It is very important that the warp is taut or the carpet will not lie flat.

Start by weaving a header with the same yarn as the warp, using a weft-faced tabby structure. Use two colours

Fig. 39   Profile Draft – 2 Block

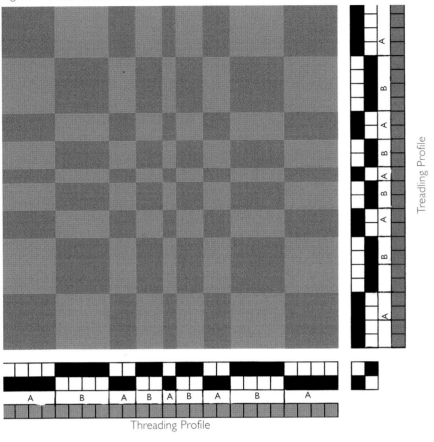

Treadling Profile

Threading Profile

of fine chenille for the weft on separate shuttles. Following the treadling draft provided (or one you have designed) start weaving the pattern blocks. Use alternate colours as many times as it takes to build up the required block length. Finish with a second hand of weft-faced tabby and weave some spacer yarn before starting your second carpet. When you have woven the carpet(s) cut them from the loom and finish the ends before gently washing. Dry flat. When dry, gently brush up the pile.

Fig. 40   Threading and Treadling Draft –
2 Block Profile

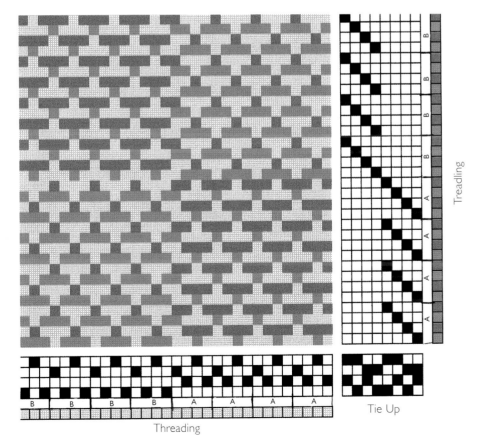

Treadling

Tie Up

Threading

WOVEN SILK TABLECLOTH

This project is designed for readers with some weaving experience and a suitable loom. The silk tablecloth shown above is made from 160/2 silk with 373 ends at 63 ends per inch, sleyed three per dent in a 21 dents per inch reed. The cloth is 7⅜in wide on the loom and 5in wide when finished. The weft is 160/2 silk at 56ppi. If you do not have any weaving experience, make a cloth to fit your table following the instructions for the table cover used for the Tudor feast (page 25).

Refer to Fig. 43 on pages 116-117. Beginning and ending with three ends thread 2, 1, 2 for selvedge, weave the cloth with a draw as follows:

A x 4, B, C, D, E, F, G, H, I, J, K, L, M, N, M, L, K, J, L, M, N, M, L, K, J, I, H, G, F, E, D, C, B, A x 4.

A tablecloth woven to 8½in on the loom will have a finished length of 7¾in. Use a hemstitch to secure the fringe, working bands of six at a time.

COTTAGE STYLE CURTAINS

For most domestic interiors during the 1930s curtains were usually fairly simple and hung to a shorter length than before but it was also popular to add a pelmet in matching fabric as shown here. To make the curtains and pelmet you will need fabric, a Pretty Pleater, spray starch, bonding fabric, glue, matching thread and a curtain pole.

Make the curtains in the same way as the velvet curtains in the Stuart drawing room (page 28). For the pelmet take a strip of fabric about 1in wide by one and a half times the width of the window. Turn under the long edges of this strip by ¼in on each side, then turn the ends under. Using the Pretty Pleater, pleat the strip and spray with starch to hold its shape (see page 161). When dry remove from the pleater and stretch to the width of the window, gluing it over the top of the curtains.

Alternatively, make a wooden pelmet top by gluing a piece of ½in wood as wide as the window to the wall above the window, then stick the curtains and pleated pelmet strip to its facing edge.

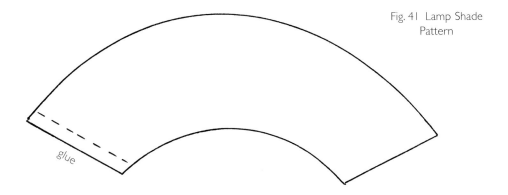

Fig. 41 Lamp Shade
Pattern

glue

 ## LAMP SHADE

The standard lamp in the corner of the room features an elegant lamp shade trimmed along the top and bottom edges with lightweight braid. The shade is easy to make from paper or thin card covered with silk or cotton fabric. The braid is optional but it is useful for covering the edges and provides a very neat finish.

All you have to do to make the shade is cut the shape of the shade from paper or thin card using the pattern above. Cut a piece of thin silk or cotton the same size, aligning one of the straight edges of the pattern with the fabric grain and glue it on top of the card. Curl the shade into shape so that the straight ends overlap to the broken line and glue together. Trim the top and bottom edges with lightweight braid if desired.

ANTIMACASSAR, MATS AND RUNNER

All homes in the 1930s would have had antimacassars on the chairs to protect them from the Macassar hair oil which men used to make their hair smooth and shiny. These antimacassars were often made from cotton with a lace edging but they were sometimes crocheted too, like the ones in this room setting. Table runners and mats made in the same way were also popular at the time as in the previous era. These four crocheted pieces have been designed by Yvonne Hodson. Yvonne used Gütermann silk and .60 crochet hook to make all four

Abbreviation	
ch = chain	rep = repeat
dc = double crochet	vst = V stitch
tr = treble crochet	sp = space
slst = slip stitch	

ANTIMACASSAR

Make this antimacassar from silk thread as follows. (If you do not have any crochet skills then you can make an antimacassar from a piece of cotton or linen, cutting it carefully on the grain and then neatly hemming around the edges. Add a fine lace or braid trim around the edges. Alternatively, use a small-patterned lace fabric to make the whole antimacassar.)

For the crocheted antimacassar shown start by making a 32ch. 1 tr into 3rd ch from hook; 1ch, miss 1ch, dc into next ch; (1ch miss 1ch, 1tr, into next ch) 10 times; 1ch miss 1ch dc into next ch; 1ch, miss 1ch, tr into last 2ch. Turn. 2ch, tr into next tr, 3ch, (miss 1ch, 1 dc 1ch)1tr into next tr, 1ch, 1tr 4 times; 1tr into 1ch space, 1tr into tr, 1ch 1tr 4 times; 3ch, (miss 1, ch1 dc 1ch) tr into last 2tr.

Work from the chart for the centre pattern and alternate 1ch, 1dc, 1ch with 3ch miss 1ch for the lacy edge. Fringe at starting chain to finish.

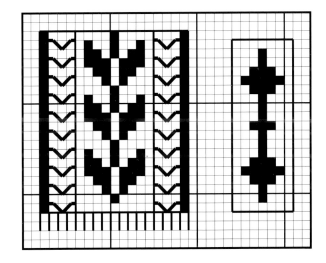

Fig 42 Crochet chart for the antimacassar and table runner (p118)

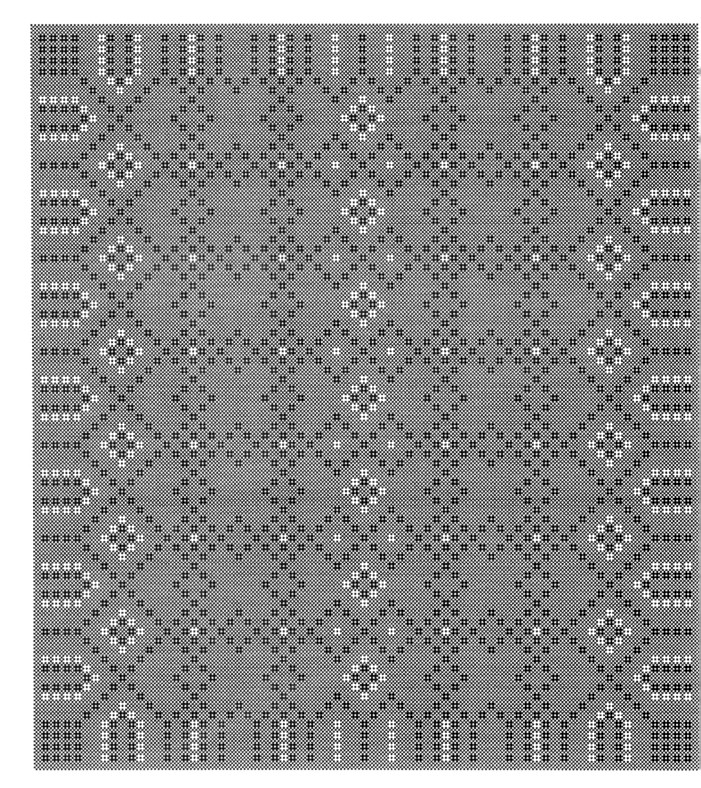

Fig. 43 Woven tablecloth designed by Bonni Backe

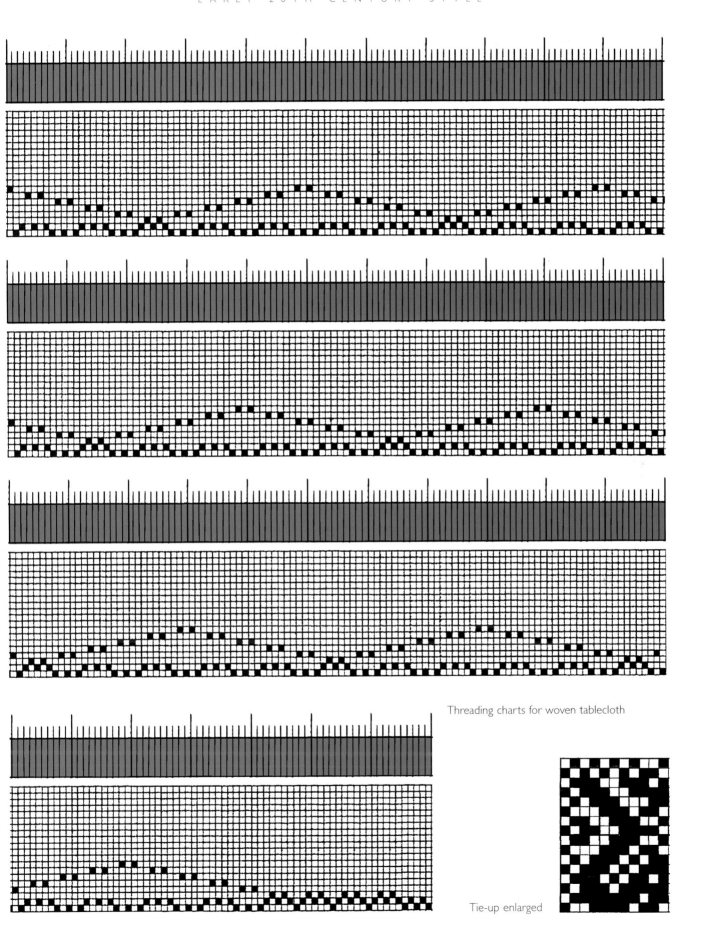

Threading charts for woven tablecloth

Tie-up enlarged

 ROUND TABLE MAT

The round mat, shown above, uses the same design as the table runner and is equally quick to make. As before use Gütermann silk and a .60 crochet hook. Refer to the abbreviations on page 115.

Commence with 4ch, slst into first ch to form a ring. 2ch, 17 tr into ring, slst into 2nd of 2ch. 4ch, tr into next tr, (2ch tr into next tr) 17 times, slst into 2nd of 4ch. 5ch, tr into next tr, (3ch tr into next tr) 17 times, slst into 3rd of 5 ch. 4ch, tr into tr 4ch stands on, (1tr 2ch 1tr into next tr) 17 times, slst into 2nd of 4 ch and into 2ch space. 4ch, tr into 2ch space, (1ch, 1tr 2ch 1tr 1ch) into 2ch space 17 times, slst into 2nd of 4ch and into 2ch space. 4ch, 1tr into 2ch space, 1ch, 1dc into 1ch, 1ch, 1tr 2ch 1tr into 2ch space) 17 times ending 1ch, slst to 2nd of 4ch. Fasten off.

OVAL MAT

Make this pretty oval mat as part of the crocheted set for the living room. As before use Gütermann silk and a .60 crochet hook.

Make 17ch, 1tr into 8th ch, ★2ch, miss 2ch, 1tr into next ch,★ (rep from ★ to ★ once) 2ch, miss 2ch, 1tr into last ch, 2ch turn. 2tr into 2ch sp, 1tr into tr 3 times, 9tr into end loop, 1tr into bottom of tr, 2tr into 2ch space twice, 1tr into tr, 6tr into space slst to first 2ch. 4ch, 1tr into same place as slst, ★miss 2tr in next tr work as vst of 1tr 2ch 1tr★ rep 3 times; (miss 1tr vst in next tr) rep () once, then rep from ★ to ★ 4 times, miss 1tr vst in next tr and slst to 3rd of 5ch, 12 vst. Slst into vst 2ch, 4tr into vst, ★dc into sp between vst, 5tr into vst ★ rep ★ to ★ 10 times, slst to 2ch. Fasten off.

 TABLE RUNNER

This table runner uses the same design as the anti-macassar in the 1930s living room. As before, use Gütermann silk and a .60 crochet hook.

Commence with 19ch. 1tr into 7th ch, 1ch miss 1ch 1tr into next ch, to end turn. 3ch, miss 1ch 1tr into next tr, 1ch miss 1ch, 1tr into next tr twice, 1tr into 1ch, sp, 1tr into next tr, 1ch miss 1ch, 1tr into next tr to end turn. Follow the chart on page 115 to the end and repeat it if you want a longer runner. Dc evenly all the way round and fasten off.

118

1930s BEDROOM

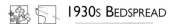 1930s BEDSPREAD

The typical 1930s bedroom would have been decorated in subtle shades of beige, orange and gold. Walls would have been papered and embellished with a border of geometric or other fashionable design. Woodwork was often painted or of light oak or walnut while fabrics used for furniture and furnishings were cotton, often printed with brightly coloured geometric designs or plain satins with leather or fur popular for upholstery. Patterned rugs of wool or animal skins were used for the floor. Although we have not fitted out a bedroom from this era, we have made a bedspread to get you started. Needlecrafts were increasingly popular at this time, especially amongst stay-at-home housewives, and this type of bedspread would have been highly desirable.

This bedspread, designed by Jill Swift, is worked in simple crewel embroidery stitches over an existing pattern printed on fabric. It could be made for a single or double bed. If you are not a confident embroiderer you can simply omit the stitching.

To make the bedspread you will need fabric which has a small printed pattern. Some cotton patchwork materials are suitable for this project. You will also need matching thread, silk or fine cotton for backing, stranded embroidery cotton in suitable colours, a circular embroidery frame and an embroidery needle.

Measure the bed (single or double), allowing for the bedclothes and the drop to the floor. Make a pattern from your measurements and add ½in all round for turnings. If

The off-white colour which dominates this room gives it an air of
luxury which was inspired by the glamorous scenes in Hollywood
movies of the day.

you are using an embroidery frame it may be necessary to attach the printed material to a larger piece of fine muslin to accommodate the frame (see page 157). You can embroider through this second layer or cut it away at the back if you prefer.

This particular piece was embroidered using two strands of stranded embroidery cotton in order to cover the printed design effectively. This may vary depending on the design of your fabric. Stitches used were detached chain, stem stitch and French knots (see page 158). Simply use your chosen embroidery stitches to outline the designs on the fabric and add embellishment where you see fit.

When all the pattern has been embroidered lay it out face down on a towel to prevent the stitches being squashed and press it. Turn and press ½in to the back on all edges. Cut lining material just a fraction smaller than the main bedspread before the turnings were pressed. Press ½in to the wrong side all round, then pin the lining and bedspread together with wrong sides facing and stitch together all round with very small slipstitches.

HOLLYWOOD BEDROOM

During the 1940s and early 1950s Hollywood movies showed another world of glamour, romance and sophistication which had a huge influence on many aspects of design including interior decoration. This room has been built to incorporate these features and is finished in tones of white. The matching bed, tall boy, bed-side cupboards, dressing table and stool are made in miniature to represent a set produced in America in the late 1940s. We sprayed them off-white and recovered the stool to give them the required look for our Hollywood room. The wallpaper is also off-white with a small design in gold and the carpet runs from wall to wall.

The large window is dressed with a plain white sheer fabric which drops from behind a coving and the skirting board, lamp shade, light fitting and bedspread are also finished in white. The use of an accent colour – in this case bright red – really brings the room to life as does the splendid figure created by doll artist James Carrington.

Soft furnishings in this room comprise a white silk quilt worked entirely in running stitch or backstitch, drapes, luxury carpet and the lamp shade.

 ## 1950s DRAPES

The curtain that covers the entire back wall of this bedroom has been made from a single piece of lightweight cotton fabric. The actual fabric used measures twice the width of the wall by the height plus turnings. To make it you will need fabric, a Pretty Pleater, some spray starch, fusible bonding fabric such as Bondaweb, multi-purpose glue and a curtain pole or other support to hang the curtain in place. Simply follow the instructions for the velvet curtain in the Stuart drawing room, joining pieces of fabric if necessary to make up the required width (see page 28).

LUXURIOUS CARPET

Make a fluffy pile carpet from a fur fabric designed for toys or children's costumes. Look for a fabric with a fairly short pile that will be in scale with the size of your dolls' house. Cut it to the shape of the room and glue in place in the same way as the carpet in the Regency salon (see page 69). Fur fabric is knitted so it does not fray. This means that there is no need to tuck under a seam allowance around the edges of, say, a hearth. Simply cut the fabric to shape and fit it. Glue in place if necessary. Fit the skirting board after you have laid the carpet to cover the raw fabric edges.

 ## LAMP SHADE

Make the shade for this room using the pattern given for the shade in the 1930s living room (see page 115) but omit the braid trim. All you need is paper or thin card, scissors, silk or cotton fabric and multi-purpose glue. If

fold line

Fig. 44 White Quilt Design

you are making the white quilt you can use fabric left-over from that project for a co-ordinated look.

WHITE QUILT

Dora Lockyer created this traditional wholecloth quilt from a piece of fine white silk and two pieces of cotton lawn each approximately 12 x 9in. She created the design on paper first and then transferred it to fine silk by tracing with a sharp pencil. She then hand stitched the design with a fine needle and silk thread. The whole design is worked in running stitch or backstitch so you do not need any advanced sewing skills to stitch it. To make your own wholecloth quilt you will need tracing paper, ordinary masking tape, fine silk fabric, cotton lawn, a sharp pencil, tacking (basting) thread and fine white silk thread.

First photocopy the design and tape it to a firm surface such as a drawing board or table top. Place the fine silk on top of the photocopy and tape it securely in position. With a sharp pencil trace the design onto the silk fabric using tiny dashes to create a broken line. When the design has been transferred make a quilt sandwich with the fine silk on top of the two pieces of lawn. Tack the three layers together securely. Now you are ready to quilt the panels. Work the centre panel of shells first with small backstitch or running stitch, if preferred, and then outline the panel with the same stitch. When you have finished quilting the centre panel work the two side panels and finish each with an outline.

To finish the quilt trim the middle piece of lawn to the fold line. Then trim the top silk fabric and the backing piece to about ⅜in from the fold line. Fold the edges in so the folds are on the fold lines and tack the folds in place just inside the edge. Tack the layers together ensuring that the edges are level. Work a line of stitching all round the design about ¼in from the edge. Finally, stitch another line all round the quilt approximately ⅛in from the edge. Remove the tacking threads when all the stitching is finished.

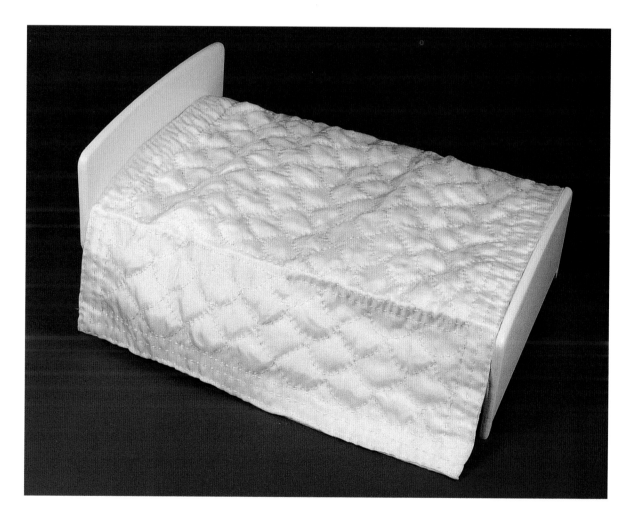

CONTEMPORARY LIVING

The 1960s and 1970s saw an experimentation with new materials such as moulded foam rubber, plastics and synthetic fibres and yet also a fondness for the natural materials of unpolished wood and leather and textured natural fibre fabrics like hessian in earthy tones of browns and terracotta. Modern Scandinavian design became popular which led to open plan rooms, often with heavy use of white but with accents of deep blue or orange. Timber-clad feature walls and furniture laminated in white or more often teak wood finish were popular as were bold colours and strong textures but rarely patterned surfaces. Curtains, carpets and upholstery fabrics were usually of solid colour. Form was given to the room by the shape of the objects held within it. This led to an interior design style often referred to as high tech which is largely still with us today. Initially the style borrowed concepts from the sophisticated industrial age and featured materials such as bricks, concrete, glass, iron and steel and rubber workroom flooring in more or less raw, undecorated form. Now it takes its lead from the age of computers and technological communication.

This modern living space in a converted warehouse has kitchen units by E. L. F. and furniture from IKEA. Minimal soft furnishings in neutral colours complete the look.

The 1990s and early twenty-first century have brought a 'want it all and want it now' outlook which in many ways is reflected in interior design, much as it was for the Victorians. Many desire the most from the modern world and through their homes want to show that they have 'arrived'. Now every influence from the past is rehashed in decoration intended to give an air of comfort and luxury, perhaps even opulence and sophistication. Nevertheless, there is regard for the past and appreciation of life gone by. The interest in antiques and the antique look of homes has never been more popular. We love the look of the past but bring it in either larger or smaller doses into our modern homes. For soft furnishings we now have every conceivable variety of material at our disposal from traditional silks, velvets and brocades to easy-to-wash, easy-to-iron synthetics. Currently interior decoration colour preferences and favoured styles change almost with the season, although perhaps that is nothing new.

MODERN LIVING SPACE

Modern living space is about just that – living space. With so many more people working and entertaining at home the need for a flexible environment appears to be today's requirement. Loft living has become enviable, particularly amongst the young and fashionable and as more people live either alone or in less conventional family units this kind of space seems ideal. We imagine that this room is a converted space within a Thames-side warehouse. Furnishings are minimal and at the same time stylish. Materials are natural: wood, brick, plaster and stainless steel and soft furnishing colours are neutral.

Our room has been constructed within a room box which measures 2½in wide, 12in deep and 11½in high but the floor of one half has been raised by nearly ½in for a separate kitchen area. The back wall and ceiling are painted a brilliant white and the side walls are covered with miniature brick cladding. The floor is of wood strip boarding. Kitchen units are also of natural wood finish with chrome handles and stainless steel work surfaces. The cooker hood and matching fire flue are also stainless steel. Somewhat fittingly the sofa and coffee table come from a miniature set by IKEA, the full sized home furnishing company, but we have sprayed them a metallic silver and made our own cushions for the sofa. The imaginary owners, created by doll artist James Carrington, have collected pieces of ancient Egyptian artefacts, which are displayed on simple painted open shelves, and old Roman glassware in illuminated cabinets along the back wall.

Soft furnishings in this type of space are minimal — the sofa cushions, leather bar stool covers, plain place mats and woven kitchen towels.

FITTED SOFA CUSHIONS

New no-sew upholstered cushions have been made for this toy dolls' house sofa to give it better scale. If you wish to do the same you will need ⅛in balsa wood, suitable fabric and glue.

From ⅛in balsa wood cut two back cushions 2½ x 1½in, two seat cushions 2½ x 2in and two end cushions 2 x 1½in. Cut fabric large enough to cover the front of each one with enough to wrap onto the back and use it to wrap the wood: we cut two pieces 3½ x 2½, two pieces 3½ x 3 and two pieces 3 x 2½in. Wrap each block with its corresponding piece of fabric and glue the edges of the fabric securely on the reverse side of each piece. When dry glue the side, back and then the seat cushions in place on the sofa.

SQUAB CUSHIONS

To complete the look of the sofa make squab cushions in the same way as those displayed in the window recess of the Arts & Crafts parlour (see page 92). We made ours from the same fabric as the sofa cushions for an understated look which suits this room scheme.

BAR STOOL COVERS

The stools beside the breakfast bar have soft leather covers which complement the natural fabrics used here. To recover bar stools like this simply cut leather large enough to go over the top of each stool and round to the base. Stretch the leather over the rounded top and glue it underneath each stool. Trim off any excess material for a neat finish.

PLACE MATS

To help to set the scene for our imaginary couple we have placed some items on the breakfast bar including fruit, a bottle of wine and so on. There are also some place mats to protect the wooden surface which are easily made from loosely woven upholstery or curtain fabric.

Simply cut a 1½ x 1¼in rectangle of fabric for each place mat required. Fray each edge by about an ⅛in by carefully pulling out the cross threads and apply liquid Fray Check to prevent further fraying, if desired. Press with a hot iron.

WOVEN TEA TOWELS

If you do not have weaving skills you can make some tea towels in the same way as the place mats using fine checked fabric, but if you do have a loom and some weaving skills then you will love these simple designs by Bonni Backe. Bonni works on full-size floor looms. They are faster to weave on than table looms because your feet do the harness changing while your hands keep hold of the shuttle, but all Bonni's patterns can be woven on table looms. She recommends buying a fine reed — the coarsest she uses for miniatures is 15 dents per inch.

For the warp use 60/2 cotton in a natural colour, 50/3 in dark blue and 47/3 in scarlet. The warp length should be 2yds and the width 2½in. The set is 60 epi and the reed is No. 20 with a sley of 3 per dent. There are 136 ends. Use the same yarn for the weft woven at 56 picks per inch, off tension.

Fig. 45 Tea Towels Weaving Diagram

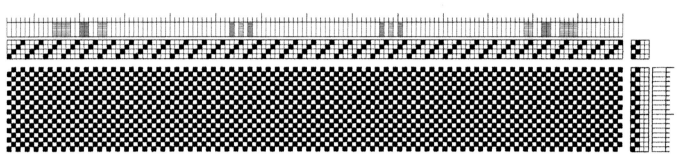

Weaving instructions:

Warp:

60/2 cotton, natural	10		2	2	27	1	1	28	1	1	27	2	2	10			
50/3 dark blue			2		1		1	1	1		1		2				
47/3 scarlet		4		2		1			1		2		4				

Weft:

For the striped tea towel: 60/2 cotton, natural, solid for 3½in

For the end stripe tea towel:

60/2 cotton, natural	½in	2	2	2in	2	2	½in	
50/3 dark blue			2			2		
47/3 scarlet		3		2	2		3	

For the window-pane tea towel:

60/2 cotton, natural	½in	2	2	24	1	1	24	1	1	24	1	1	24	2	2	½in
50/3 dark blue			2		1	1	1		1	1	1		1			
47/3 scarlet		3	2		1		1			1		1		2	3	

To finish mark the towels at 2⅞in with a disappearing ink marker. Stay with the grain of the fabric as much as possible. If you are making a number of towels at one time leave ¼in between the towels for the fringe. If preferred, this allowance may be slightly more on the towels with filling stripes. Using 60/2 cotton and a No 9 (70) sewing machine needle, stitch along the drawn line, using a stitch length of ⅜in. Cut the towels apart between the stitching. Unravel the filling down to the stitching, being very careful not to pull out the stitching. The weaving is quite fragile at this stage. Wash the towels in washing-up liquid and hot water, then rinse. Roll up in a towel to remove excess water and iron dry. Trim the fringe using a rotary cutter or sharp scissors.

NOTE: When changing filling colours do not weave the ends back in. Just leave the colours looping out along the selvedges and then trim them off evenly with the towel after you have ironed them.

GARDEN ROOM

Conservatories, sun rooms, covered patios or garden rooms, call them what you will, from the 1990s onwards these rooms have become increasingly popular. Ours is given a pretty garden feel with floral patterned fabrics and the use of grapes and vines. The basic colour for the room is green mixed with the pinky mauves of the grapes and flowers which helps to create a natural feel. The white planked ceiling and black and white tiled floor help to continue the outdoor look.

The table and its covers, chair covers, pelmet and matching wall frieze have all been conceived by a top miniaturist working in this field, d. Anne Ruff. She made the curtain and main tablecloth from plain green fabric and the top table cover, seat cushions, pelmet and wall frieze from a tiny print floral design. Use fabrics of your choice to copy the look.

CIRCULAR TABLE

The elegant round table in the conservatory, complete with its floor-length covers, can be made from scratch using card and fabric. The base is completely covered but it is sturdy enough to support not just the drapes but any items you wish to add on top. The two table covers can be made using any fabrics which suit your room, although a plain fabric works best for the bottom cover.

X TABLE BASE

This sturdy table base has a strong central X support made from two interlocking pieces of card plus a circular base and top and an outer cover made from a role of card so it will not wobble or collapse. Use thin card or poster board to make it and use paper to cover the top and bottom. You will also need glue and a craft knife.

First cut the table base (A) on page 130 from thin card or poster board. Mark on the glue lines then roll the card into a tube with the glue lines on the outside – pressing it with a warm iron will soften the cardboard and allow it to be more easily rolled into shape. Overlap the end flaps and glue as marked, holding the cardboard until the glue has dried or using tape to secure it. Cut two table supports from card or board, one from pattern B and one from C and score along the broken lines. Fold

The soft furnishing projects in this ornate garden room really help to create the look yet they are all quite quick and simple to produce.

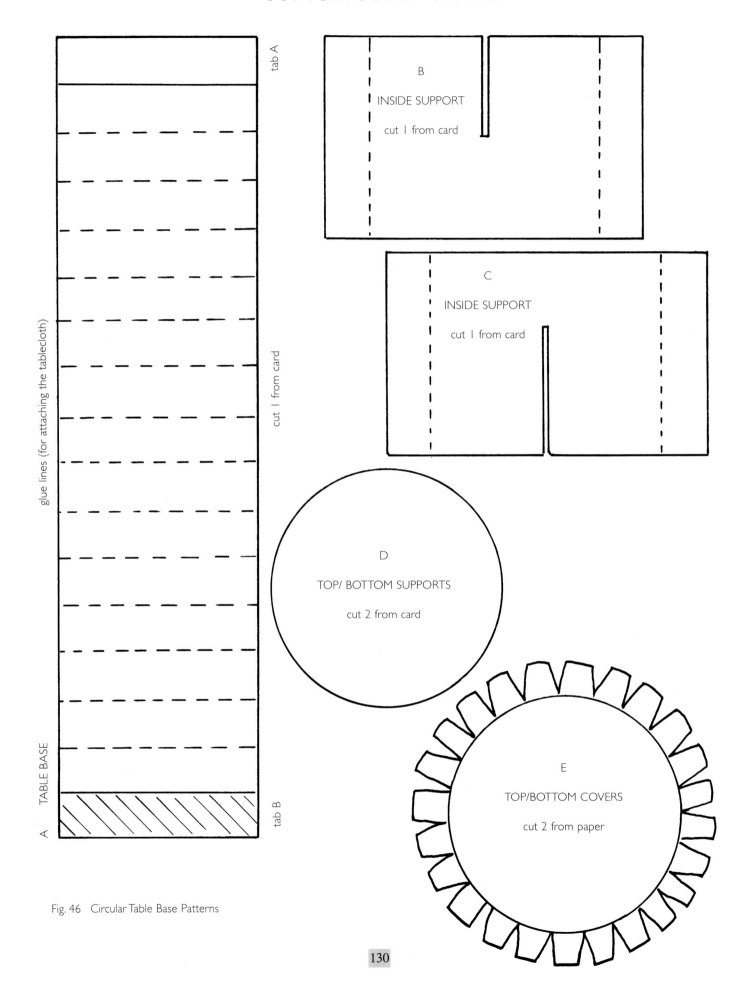

tab A

glue lines (for attaching the tablecloth)

cut 1 from card

tab B

A   TABLE BASE

B

INSIDE SUPPORT

cut 1 from card

C

INSIDE SUPPORT

cut 1 from card

D

TOP/ BOTTOM SUPPORTS

cut 2 from card

E

TOP/BOTTOM COVERS

cut 2 from paper

Fig. 46   Circular Table Base Patterns

the card along the scored lines then insert support B into the cardboard tube (A). Slide support C into the slot in B, creating an X support. It is not necessary to glue these pieces in place.

Now cut two circles from thin card/poster board using pattern D and cut two circles from paper using pattern E. Centre a card/poster board circle inside each paper circle and glue it in place. Fold the slashed tabs up around the edge of the cardboard circles. Put a dot of glue on the inside of these tabs and on the exposed edges of the inner table supports and glue the paper covered circles in place on the top and bottom of the card tube (A). Leave to dry thoroughly. Your table base is now complete.

 TABLECLOTH

This full floor-length tablecloth covers the table base and gives it a very elegant look. We used plain green fabric for the cover which co-ordinates with the colour of the plant stand in the corner of the room. Ideally use a plain fabric too because the cloth is cut from one piece of fabric so any pattern will hang upside down on one side. You will need fabric, muslin, fusible webbing such as Bondaweb, paper, multi-purpose glue, paper glue or glue stick and a toothpick, dowel or pencil.

Cut an 8in square of fabric for the tablecloth and an 8in square of muslin (or other lightweight piece of cotton) for the lining, and fuse them together with fusible webbing, following the manufacturer's instructions. Use the pattern below to draw a 7in diameter circle on paper and cut it out. Cut out the centre of the circle as indicated and discard. Spread a thin layer of white glue on the back of the paper ring (or use a glue stick or fusible webbing) and press it in place (printed lines up) on the lining side of the fabric. Cut away excess fabric around the outer edge of the circle, leaving about ¼in of fabric all round for a hem. Spread a thin line of glue on this edge of the fabric and turn back over the edge of the paper ring. Press in place with an iron.

With the paper side out, fold the skirt in half along the first glue line indicated by a broken line on the pattern. Press each line in this way so that there is a fold along each one. Spread a thin layer of glue over the top of the table base, then place the table base upside down into the cut-out centre of the skirt, matching the folds in the skirt with the glue lines on the table base. Press down firmly to secure. Turn the table right side up and press the top lightly with an iron.

Place the table upside down again and run a thin ribbon of glue along each glue line on the table base.

Fig. 47 Tablecloth Pattern

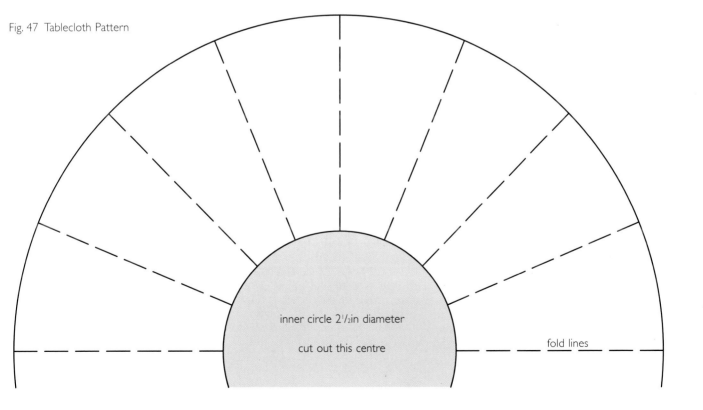

inner circle 2½in diameter

cut out this centre

fold lines

Cut a 4½in square of co-ordinating fabric or muslin. Be sure that the cut edges are on the grain. Begin pulling out cross threads on each edge until you have a ¼in fringe. Next, cut a 4in square of fusible interfacing and fuse onto the back of the fabric. It should not extend into the fringe area.

Cover the top of the table with a thin layer of glue. Lay out the cover, face down, and centre the table on top; press firmly. Spread glue on the remainder of the cover on the wrong side, turn the table right side up and press the cover fabric evenly down into the folds.

CHAIR SEAT CUSHIONS

The bistro chairs beside the circular table feature pretty squab seat cushions tied onto the back of the chairs in typical country style. They are made from the same floral fabric as the table cover and the wall frieze. To make them you will need paper, thin card, thin foam rubber or an alternative padding, fabric, glue and ribbon or cord.

Lay paper over one of the chair seats and press round it to mark the edges. Draw along the creases to mark out your pattern then trace the pattern onto a piece of thin card. Cut a piece of thin foam rubber or other padding slightly larger than the card and glue it on the card. Fit the padded card on the seat and trim it to match exactly, if necessary. Next cut a piece of fabric slightly larger than padded cushion and spread glue on the back or use fusible webbing. Place the fabric over the padding and turn over all raw edges to the back. Press the edges with your fingers to secure them (or fuse in place if using webbing). Glue the seat cushion in place on the chair and add ribbon or cord ties to the back of the chair.

SCALLOPED PELMET

The window has a scalloped pelmet which matches the wallpaper border for a truly co-ordinated look. To make it you will need lightweight card, glue, fusible webbing (such as Bondaweb) and fabric.

Trace all three pelmet patterns onto lightweight cardboard such as that from a file folder. Cut out the pieces and pre-fold along the broken lines marked on the patterns. Glue the stabiliser (B) onto the back of the pelmet frame (A), matching the curves. Cut a piece of fabric ¼in larger all round than the frame (A) and cut a piece of fusible webbing the same size as the frame (A).

Carefully bring up the skirt fabric along one of the folded lines and press the fold line into the glue line on the base. Make sure the skirt edge is even with the bottom of the base. Press in place with a finger until secure or use a dressmakers' pin at the edge to hold it in place. Continue bringing up each fold and holding or pinning in place until firm. You may need to add more glue if the first glue application has dried. The last couple of folds will be the most difficult to put into place. Use a toothpick, dowel or pencil to help you push them into position.

TABLE COVER

This table cover gives a pleasing finish to the table and helps coordinate it with the room scheme. We made it in the same fabric as the wall frieze. To make it all you need is a small amount of fabric or muslin, some fusible interfacing and glue.

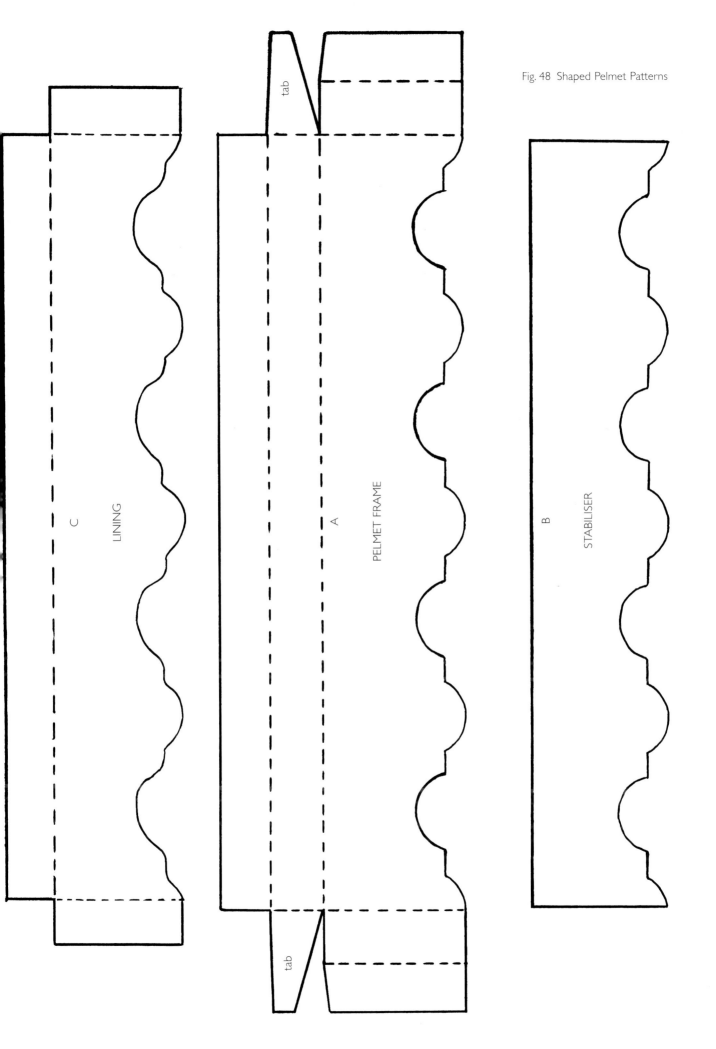

Fig. 48 Shaped Pelmet Patterns

C

LINING

tab

A

PELMET FRAME

tab

B

STABILISER

Iron the fusible webbing to the back of the fabric, peel away the paper and then fuse the fabric to the card frame.

Cut the fabric flush with all edges of the frame except the curved bottom edge where you should leave a ¼in margin. Cut along the angled edge of the tabs, leaving a triangular piece of fabric to be folded down and pressed over the side flaps. Now slash the fabric allowance along the shaped edge with cuts pointing towards the points of the curves. These cuts should not go all the way up to the frame edge. Press the triangular portions of fabric over the top edges of the flaps then turn the slashed edges back along the curves and points. Press carefully.

Spread glue along the back of the top flap. Fold down along the scored line and press until secure. Now fold over the fabric covered flap again and press with an iron to ensure a crisp fold along the top front edge of the finished cornice. Spread glue along the inside of the double side fold, fold down the triangular side flaps and bring the glued double flap around them. Make sure that this folded corner shows a sharp right angle on the outside of the corner. Lay the pelmet on its side and press the flap securely inside. Finally, spread glue on one side of the lining (C) and glue in place inside the pelmet, matching curves.

X DECORATIVE FRIEZE

Wallpaper borders have been a popular addition to many room schemes in recent years, particularly where the home owners like to create a complete look and have a soft spot for the designs of the past. In our room set the frieze matches the pelmet to continue the design around the room. It is 1½in deep. To make it all you need is thin paper, fabric, fusible webbing such as Bondaweb and sharp scissors plus a craft knife and ruler.

First determine the length of border you need for each wall by measuring it. Trace the scalloped border pattern design from the pelmet stabiliser (B) on page 133 onto thin paper, repeating the pattern as needed for the length of each wall – you will find it easier to make the borders slightly longer than necessary to help you match the pattern around the pelmet and in the corners. Cut strips of fabric about 2in wide and the length required for each wall. Iron fusible webbing onto the back of each strip of border fabric. Peel away the backing paper and press the fabric onto the back of the paper border pattern. Press very slowly, making sure the fabric is securely bonded to the paper pattern. Now use scissors to cut the curved edge of the border following the pattern outline and working from the paper side. Cut the top straight edge of the border – ideally use a craft knife and ruler.

The fabric border can now be glued in place on your wall just as you would hang a paper border. Because the cut edge is bonded to paper it should not fray. If there is a stray loose thread, touch it with a small amount of glue and pat it in place. Try to match the curve of the border with the curve of the pelmet where the two will meet and aim to make the best possible join at the corners.

DESIGNER BATHROOM

The overall look of this luxurious bathroom suggests that a professional interior designer has played a hand. Today's bathrooms and kitchens are regarded as two of the most important rooms in the home and they are given a lot of attention when it comes to the fittings and decorations. The modern bathroom is seen as somewhere that should be a comfortable retreat, a place to relax, away from other household pressures.

A very feminine look has been achieved in this spacious dolls' house bathroom. It is dominated by pink roses both in the pattern on the wallpaper and in the light fitting as well as pots and containers around the walls. The wash basin is set within a pretty vanity unit and the oval bath is sunk into a raised floor while a real touch of luxury is added by the floor to ceiling mirrors around the bath. Bath, lavatory and shower unit are also present and a huge open shelf unit on the left holds towels and several other bathroom essentials.

This room is 18in wide, 12in deep and 9½in high with false walls positioned to accommodate the shower area and both a raised floor and a lowered ceiling. The walls are mostly wallpapered with the exception of the large mirror panels around the bath and the floor is fully carpeted. Most of the ceiling is painted white but for an attractive touch the lowered part is papered to match the walls.

Soft furnishings in this room comprise the shower curtain, luxury fitted carpet and soft towels plus a simple window blind which is not featured in the main room set.

This modern bathroom has co-ordinated furnishings including the shower curtain, carpet and towels which help to give it a real-life feel.

SHOWER CURTAIN

In order to co-ordinate the pattern of the shower curtain with that of the wallpaper we photocopied a sample of the wallpaper and had it printed onto cotton fabric using the same process used for the photocopied wall hanging in the Elizabethan bedroom (page 21). You will also need an ⅛in wooden or plastic dowel, spray starch and some matching thread.

Cut a piece of fabric double the width of the shower opening by the height plus ½in added at the top. (If you are not using photocopied fabric add a little extra for a bottom hem as your fabric will fray.) Turn over the ½in top allowance, stitch in place and press. Do not stitch the ends closed. Thread an ⅛in wooden or plastic dowel the

width of the shower opening through the top of the curtain, then gather the fabric into pleats and spray with starch. To help create the right shape you can pin the pole and curtain into shape on a foam board if you wish. When dry, glue the pole into the top of the shower opening, allowing the curtain to fall to one side.

X BATH AND HAND TOWELS

All bathrooms require towels in at least two sizes for the bath and basin and you will probably also want a bath mat which can be made in the same way. The most important thing you need is the right fabric. Lightweight

cotton flannel works well and material taken from shoe-shine mitts is excellent both in scale and weight. You may also want very narrow coloured ribbon, machine made lace and fabric glue.

First cut your fabric to size: 3 x 1⅜in for a bath towel or 1⅝ x 1¼in for a hand towel. Fold the fabric into a towel shape so that the back edges meet in the middle and press. Lightweight cotton fabric will hold its shape. If you are using a slightly heavier fabric, fabric glue or double-sided tape may be required to hold the towels in a folded shape. Note that heavier fabric may look out of scale in your delicate bathroom setting. Trim by gluing on ribbon and lace if desired.

 WINDOW BLIND

One of the most popular forms of window dressing for a kitchen or bathroom in the late twentieth century was a decorative roller blind (not shown in the room set). This was not a new invention as plainer versions were used from about 1860. To make it you will need fabric, Fray Check or blind-making medium, thin dowel, multi-purpose glue, a small bead, thread and lace or braid.

For this non-working blind first cut a piece of fabric the same size as the window. Stop the edges fraying with Fray Check or better still a blind-making medium. Cut a piece of dowel the width of the fabric. Partly roll the top of the fabric from front to back around the dowel, gluing as you go. Glue another piece of dowel to the bottom of the fabric at the back. Trim the bottom with lace or braid and fashion a pull from thread and a bead. Finally, glue the top pole to the top of the window.

To complete the setting stack the towels on bathroom shelves, place at the edge of the bath or wash basin and hang two over the towel rails.

FITTED CARPET

The carpet shown here was cut and fitted in the same manner as the one in the Regency salon (see page 69) except that two pieces of fabric were used, meeting at the bottom of the step which leads from the raised floor level to the main level. If you put any steps in your bathroom you will probably need to use a little glue to hold the carpet in place in this area.

DESIGN CLASSICS

In this chapter we look at a number of design styles
which somehow remain ever green. We have selected
three as themes for room schemes which appear as
fresh if reproduced today as at the period of their concep-
tion and we have entitled them 'Design Classics' in the belief
that they are dateless and will always be admired. All are
relatively clean lined styles which seem to fit in with most

life styles and outlooks. The three looks we have chosen for this section are the American Colonial look which we have used in a bedroom, Larsson style which we have adopted to create a Swedish-looking living area and Shaker style which we have used for a retiring room that doubles as a bedroom and private living area. The American Colonial look is most often associated with rather naive style hand painted or stencilled paint finishes, rag rugs and, of course, patchwork quilts. Shaker style is more austere, with clean, basic lines and minimal soft furnishings, often in checked blue-and-white fabrics, while Larsson style falls somewhere in between – it shares much of the clean lines of the Shaker style but with a softer touch added through the use of frills and pretty fabrics.

❋   ❋   ❋

AMERICAN COLONIAL BEDROOM

American Colonial style is taken from the look of the homes of the early American settlers who embraced and combined the various folk arts of the countries from which they originally came and the items which they were able to reproduce themselves. The first colonists built their homes from whatever materials were available but sometimes these were painted or stained to appear as something else. In the absence of wallpapers stencils were developed or walls were painted freehand. The much-loved American patchwork quilt emerged from the inventiveness of recycling old clothes as otherwise the textiles available were mostly plain. The style as used today is often referred to as American country and employs crudely painted furniture in strong, deep colours, stencilled or painted walls, woven blankets, rag rugs and patchwork quilts.

In a room box 16½in wide, 9in deep and 9in high the top part of the walls has been prepared with copy sheets of original work by artisan Therese Bahl and the lower section and ceiling painted white. The fireplace has also been painted white and the floor is of wooden plank sheet. The overall look of the room is one which would date from the 1760s. The inclusion of the figure by Marcia Backstrom of Betsy Ross sewing the first flag of the United States of America might also help date it at around this time although it is thought that the rooms of her real home would have been more modest than this one.

Soft furnishings featured here are the quilts, mattress, bed linen, table covers and rag rugs.

This American Colonial bedroom is completed with fine patchwork quilts, rag rugs and table covers. The figure of Betsy Ross was made by Marcia Backstrom.

BEDDING

The bed with its beautiful quilt is perhaps the most important element in this room as far as soft furnishings are concerned. The bedstead itself, like most of the pieces in this room, is a collectable miniature dating from the 1970s but similar pieces in this style are still made today. To kit out the bed you will need a mattress, sheets and pillows and, of course, a patchwork quilt.

 AMERICAN QUILT

This splendid quilt is made in the traditional fashion from tiny pieces of fabric and will certainly be the making of your room setting. However, if you do not have the patience or the sewing skills for this project do not despair – make a quick quilt following the instructions overleaf.

To make this American style ½ scale quilt the designer, Pam Paget-Tomlinson, first consulted a book in

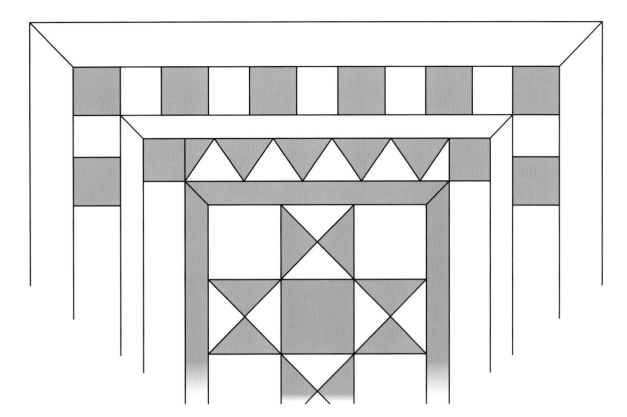

Fig. 49 American Quilt Design

her own reference library called "The American Quilt: A History of Cloth and Comfort 1750-1950" by R. Kiracofe. She decided a medallion quilt was best for the period room we were trying to create. Many quilts of this period featured a printed tree of life from India in the middle panel which was then appliquéd but as there were also pieced centre panels Pam chose an Ohio star centre-piece. To make the quilt you will need pieces of old fabric or Tana lawn (we used three fabrics), Pearsall's gossamer silk thread, fine needles, graph paper with ½in squares and thin card such as old Christmas card.

This quilt is pieced by the English method over paper or card which is easiest for small scale work. First draw the design on graph paper (see above) then glue the graph paper onto thin card and cut out the individual card templates. Use the card templates as a guide for cutting out the fabric, adding ¼in all round each one. Fold the fabric pieces over the card and tack (baste) with ordinary thread. Build the design into strips and sew the strips together, putting pins through the seams to keep lines and corners true. Do not use ordinary sewing thread for this because it is out of scale and spoils even the best work. Use a fine thread such as Pearsall's gossamer silk thread.

Once you have completed the pieced areas measure each border length and make a pattern. Cut your pattern from squared paper. Glue a spare sheet of squared paper to thin card to make templates of the plain borders. Cut out the border fabrics and stitch them to the quilt, then cut the tacking (basting) threads and remove the card from all areas of the quilt. Finally, use the pieced quilt to measure and cut a card template for the backing fabric. Add ¼in to each edge for seam allowances and cut out the fabric. Fold the backing fabric over the card and press to create sharp edges. Remove the card and pin the backing to the pieced quilt; oversew in place.

QUICK QUILTS

Extra quilts have been made for our room from printed patchwork fabric which is easily obtained from specialists selling haberdashery and fabrics suitable for dolls' houses. If you wish you can use this method to make a quilt for the bed too.

The quilt on the quilt rack is a printed piece of fabric which resembles a simple patchwork coverlet made from squares of old fabric. To make this quilt first cut a

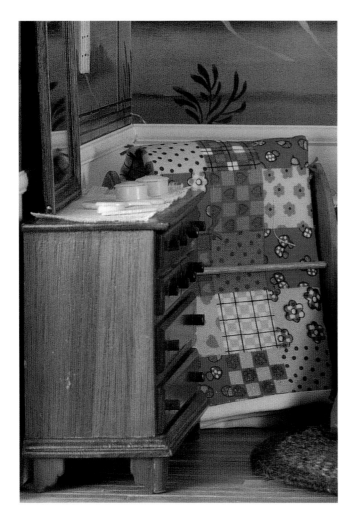

quilt an extra thin layer of soft cotton was added between the top and bottom pieces of fabric to make a traditional quilt sandwich before the borders were attached. The design of the fabric determined the finished size of the quilt – approximately 7in square. Again you can work extra quilting stitches around the designs using fine silk thread for a more authentic look, if desired.

MATTRESS

A feather mattress and cover was made for this bed in the same way as the one in the Elizabethan bedroom, page 14. We used a strong but fine cotton cambric fabric for the cover and filled it with real down feathers which were salvaged from an old feather pillow. Remember to adapt the measurements to fit a single bed.

BED LINEN

We made the sheets and pillow covers from fine Egyptian cotton. Make them in the same way as those in the Shaker retiring room (see page 151). The pillows should be plumper and look more comfortable in this setting.

TABLE COVERS

To protect the polished wooden surfaces of furniture from being scuffed by heavy objects such as jugs, lamps or candlesticks, most ladies made table covers or mats. This room features three matching table covers, one on the dresser, one on the side table and the third on the dressing table. In keeping with the style of the room they are made from plain, evenweave fabric – we used 36 count embroidery cotton. If you like you can do as we did and draw out a few threads to give the table covers a simple pattern.

To make your covers first measure the area to be covered. Our dresser was 3¾ x 1¾in so our cover was 3½ x 1½in. If you are using evenweave fabric you must cut it out on the grain and the following instructions tell you how to do this the easy way. Remove one thread near the edge of the fabric by gently pulling it. This will create a straight line for cutting. Measure the required length away and remove a second thread. Repeat across the width. Then simply cut along the channels left by the removed threads. This will ensure that your fabric is cut on the grain.

6in square of patchwork fabric and another of backing fabric. Cut strips of plain fabric approximately ½in wide and 6½in long for binding the edges. Machine sew a strip to each edge of the printed patchwork fabric with right sides facing. Next pin the patchwork fabric to the backing fabric with wrong sides facing. Fold the binding strips over the side edges and onto the backing, tucking the raw edges under neatly, and stitch in place. Now fold the end binding strips over, pin and hand sew as before. To finish use single strands of embroidery cotton to make ties in the corners of the squares. On a real bed these would secure the top worked piece to the backing. Extra quilting stitches can be added at this time too to enhance the quilt. For this, use very fine silk thread such as Pearsall's gossamer silk thread.

The quilt just visible in the blanket box has also been made from printed fabric. In this case the fabric is designed to resemble a quilt with plain squares combined with pieced squares of patchwork. The quilt was made in the same way as the one on the quilt rack but for this

To make the simple but effective pattern pull and remove two threads in the middle and approximately ¼in from the edges at the sides and both ends. Then fray the edges for ⅛in. On a smaller table cover only make channels through the middle of the fabric in both directions.

RAG RUG

Materials to make traditional braided rugs for a dolls' house vary: stranded embroidery cotton or wool, flower or mat floss, wool weaving thread or lambswool thread all work well. The most important thing is that it is very fine so it is in scale. When choosing colours for the rug you may find it helpful to refer to actual rugs detailed in reference books or on show in museums or stately homes. The rugs shown were made by Ann Miller who used three 18in strands of thread braided in fairly muted colours. Each braid is ³⁄₃₂in in diameter. As well as your chosen thread you will also need fine sewing thread, masking tape and lightweight iron-on interfacing.

For the rug make up several braided strips 18in long in mixed colours and tie off both ends. Make some braids with three dark colours, some with light colours, some mixed with light and dark and others from neutral colours such as cream or brown. The number of braided strips will depend on how large the finished rug is to be.

To assemble the rug take a 4in long strip of 2in wide masking tape and the braided strip chosen for the centre of the rug. Stick one end of the braid to the centre of the masking tape and then fold the braid, doubling it back beside the first part in a U-shape. The first section of braid should be 2-3in long. Begin at the fold and with a blunt needle lace the two sections of braid together. Note: the top of the rug will be against the sticky side of the masking tape. Continue working in this way.

To change the colour of the braid tie off the old braid and stitch securely to the back of the rug. Start a new strip by securing the end to the back of the rug and proceed as before. As strips of braid are added you will come to the edge of the masking tape. Add more masking tape, overlapping the previous section of tape by about ½in. Keep working in this way until the rug is the required size. Lace the braid strips together as you go.

When the stitching is complete secure the final end to the back of the rug as before. Trim all tails on the back of the rug to reduce bulk, then lightly steam the back of the rug with your iron to make it lie flat. To reinforce the rug and help it to lie flat use the completed rug as a pattern to cut a piece of lightweight iron-on interfacing and fuse it to the back of the rug. Steaming causes the rug to be released from the masking tape. Turn the rug right side up and press firmly. Peel off the tape to finish.

LARSSON STYLE ROOM

Carl and Karin Larsson have been dubbed the creators of the Swedish style. This is perhaps going a little far but certainly they turned it around and made it their own. This room is based directly on the southern side of the drawing room of the Larssons' home, Lilla Hyttnäs in Sundbon, Northwest of Stockholm as seen in water-colours dated 1894 and 1909.

Born in 1853, Carl Larsson was an artist whose best known works portrayed a light-hearted view of idyllic family life in the countryside. Together with his wife Karin (also originally an artist), he turned their home into a real-ity of this idea using creativity, practicality and humour.

This miniature room is 11¾in wide, 6½in deep and 9½in high but is built into a space 18 x 10 x 9½in to allow for a side bedroom and an area beyond the window. In accordance with reference pictures the walls have been painted an orange-yellow, with mouldings of mid-green, the ceiling is creamy white and the floor is of natural light wood boarding. The main feature of the room is the window which has been dressed with plants and ivy made by Georgina Steeds, again in keeping with the reference pictures. The dresser and the two chairs are from Charlotte Hunt Miniatures whose speciality is fur-niture of a Swedish style.

Soft furnishings in this room comprise the loose chair seat covers, the fitted box bed, table runner and tablecloth, the door hanging, rectangular carpet and rag rugs. Note the touch of authenticity in the way the woven carpet folds back on itself to change direction.

✂ LACY TABLECLOTH

This lacy tablecloth is perfectly in keeping with this room setting but it would also work well in a Victorian or Edwardian room. All you need to do to make it is cut a piece of lacy fabric to fit (we used antique lace) and then spray it with starch. Quickly, while it is still wet, lay the lace over your table and mould it into shape with your fingers. Leave it to dry naturally.

This room was modelled on the Larssons' home in Sundbon, Sweden and features a range of simple soft furnishings including the loose chair seat covers and table runner.

WOVEN RUG

This room features a woven rag rug designed and made by Ina Wichers. If you do not have a loom you can still create the rug by making your own loom following the instructions on page 162, however you will also need some basic weaving experience to make it. Alternatively, make a standard rag rug following the instructions right. To make this rug you will need assorted colours of finely woven cloth such as Liberty prints, silks, old scarves, stockings or tights and suitable thread for the warp. Cut the cloth into fine strips.

Lay the warp threads in the usual manner then start your work by weaving four or six times across with the same thread as the warp. Wind lengths of cloth strips around the shuttles, then weave back and forth from left to right, changing colours as you see fit. The pattern is the choice of the weaver, so let your creativity flow. Be careful not to pull the weft threads too tightly as this will pull the side edges in. Finish the piece by weaving four to six times across with the same thread as the warp thread. Cut the rug off the frame and tie knots in the warp threads close to the edge.

ALTERNATIVE RAG RUG

Rag rugs are just as much part of the Larsson look as the Colonial style. You can make one in the same way as the one in the Colonial bedroom (see page 143) but instead of making it round or oval make a rectangular one. Work in the same way as for the round or oval rugs, but start at one end and work to the other, laying out enough braid to reach across the full width of the rug before turning. Stitch a tiny fringed braid to the ends, if desired.

LOOSE CHAIR-SEAT COVER

Although already beautifully upholstered, Charlotte Hunt's chairs have been recovered so they are more in keeping with the Larsson style. The loose covers are made

from tiny blue and white cotton checked fabric on which each check measures approximately ½in.

To make covers like these first cut a 1¾in square of fabric (this may vary depending on the size of your chair). Then cut a strip of fabric approximately ⁵⁄₁₆in wide and 3in long for the frill. Work a line of running stitch along one long edge of the strip, leaving long tails on each end of the thread. Pull up the thread to form small, even gathers and pin it to the seat cover around three edges with right sides facing and raw edges matching. Hand sew in place. Lightly press the cover and fit it on the chair.

TABLE RUNNER

The table runner in this room was made by cutting a piece of fabric 2¼ x 7½in. Cut your fabric to fit the piece of furniture it is to cover. Fray both ends by pulling out the cross threads but apply liquid Fray Check or clear nail varnish to the underside along the long edges to prevent fraying. If you are using even-weave fabric refer to the instructions for the table covers in the American Colonial bedroom to cut it out evenly (see page 142).

FITTED BOX BED

The box bed in the adjacent room is 6 x 3in. It has been built in with separate head and foot boards butted up again the walls. For a bed cover we simply wrapped a block of 3in thick foam with a tiny red and white cotton checked fabric. Then we covered two 3in long wooden dowels, each ½in in diameter, with the same fabric to make bolsters. 'Sausage' cases were made to cover the wooden dowels and then the ends were gathered. To make the cases cut fabric 4in wide by the circumference of the dowel plus ½in. Stitch the joining edges together taking a ¼in seam allowance. Turn in the fabric ends by ¼in and work running stitch along these edges, leaving long tails of thread at each end. Pull up the running stitch on one end and knot securely. Insert the dowel, then pull up the thread at the other end and secure in the same way.

DOOR HANGING

A door hanging covers the doorway between the living room and the box bedroom for a casual, welcoming

The box bedroom adjoining the Larsson style living area is separated by a door hanging. Inside, the box bed is fitted with a bed cover and bolster pillow.

look. It was based on a hanging in the Larsson home as shown in an illustration and was made by photocopying the design onto fabric in the same way as the photocopied wall hangings in the Elizabethan bedroom (see page 21). To give the hanging some body we lightly folded it into pleats before gluing it to the top of the door frame as shown above.

SHAKER RETIRING ROOM

Currently enjoying a renewed popularity, the Shaker style is clean, simple and functional, fitting well into today's world. Originally the style evolved from a religious sect founded in America by Ann Lee in 1830–1850. Their belief was that their communal lives should be simple, well ordered and without human fault with Christ as their role model. The Shakers endeavoured to produce everything for their needs themselves, including buildings, cloth, furniture and food. Their furniture reflected their simple lives being practical, uniform and unadorned. The style is epitomised by ladder back chairs and rockers with woven seats, three legged sewing tables,

This Shaker style room was made by John Morgan and measures 10 x 9½ x 9in. Soft furnishings are in blue and white in accordance with the strict Millennial Laws. They include two woven projects – the twill blanket and rug. If you lack the necessary skills or equipment to make these just follow the instructions to make the simpler alternatives.

oval storage boxes, small single beds and rails of pegs that run around the room walls. All would be of pale wood with no ornamentation. It is rare that bedrooms would not be shared but it is possible that this miniature example represents only half of a whole room.

This room box and its contents have been collected over many years so some of the exact pieces used may

not still be available although you can buy similar items. The soft furnishings made specifically for the room are the wall cloth, bedding, towels, curtains and rug.

We followed the Millennial Laws written in 1820 to make the soft furnishing projects for this room. Formal written colour restrictions were explicit in that only three hues were permitted in retiring rooms. Only two colours – blue and white – were to be used on bed coverings, bedsteads should be painted green, while curtains were to be white, blue or green. An enormous amount of time went into the preparation, creation and upkeep of all textiles, and even though the restrictions were an attempt at standardisation they were never completely effective.

 WALL CLOTH

Wall cloths protected the walls around the beds and also acted as insulation against the cold winter winds of North America. Ours was made from fabric taken from a woven, pure cotton pillowcase found in a store selling modern products from Japan. The weave is a very fine blue and white ⅜in check on a pale tan background. You will also need lining fabric, preferably 100% cotton and ⅛in ribbon tape to make the cloth.

To make the wall cloth cut a 10 x 6½in rectangle from each fabric. (This might vary depending on the size of your retiring room.) With right sides facing, pin the two fabrics together and machine sew around three sides, taking a ¼in seam allowance. Make diagonal stitches across the corners. Leave the top edge open to insert tabs for hanging. Trim seams and corners, turn the cloth right sides out and press. Turn in the raw edges along the top of the cloth by ¼in and press again.

To make the tabs cut 1in lengths of 1/16in ribbon tape and fold them in half to make loops. Measure the distance between pegs on the peg rail and space the loops along the top of the wall cloth accordingly. Pin the loops between the top cover and lining so that ¼in protrudes at the top and put extra pins along the edge to hold it closed for sewing. Hand sew along the edge using a blind hemming stitch, securing the tabs as you do so. Press the cloth one more time and hang it on the peg rail.

Towels

The towels used by the Shakers were woven in a plain weave, either in solid colours or blue and white check or in 'huckabuck', a weave with a highly textured surface. We made towels for this room which represent all three types of fabric. We found a textured fabric to simulate huckabuck – plain cotton with a tiny blue and white check – and cut the fabric to the required size. The towels range in size. They are 1⅛ x 3¾in including fringe, 1½ x 3½in, 1½ x 2½in and 1¼ x 3¼in.

To make fringed towels simply cut your fabric to size and then tease out the cross threads from each end until the fringe is the required depth. A pin is a useful tool for this. For hemmed towels turn an ⅛in hem. We used fusible webbing slipped between the hem allowance and the main towel to fuse the hems in place but you can stitch the hems with fine thread if preferred.

Half Curtains

Shaker windows were not left bare as is the common notion about these dwellings. Instead curtains covered the lower half of the windows and were usually of plain white linen or cotton but could be green or blue. Stripes, checks or floral patterns were strictly prohibited. To make the curtains you will need a lightweight sheer cotton fabric, paper, 1/16in wide ribbon, DMC pearl cotton, a Pretty Pleater, glue and a small dowel for a pole cut to fit the window.

Measure the window and make a paper pattern to the size of the lower half of the window, adding a hem allowance of ¼in at the sides and bottom. If possible place

the top edge of the pattern on the fabric selvedge. Our pattern was 3¼ x 5½in. Cut out your fabric and hand sew double ⅛in hems along the bottom and side edges by turning the fabric over by ⅛in and then over again by another ⅛in. Glue a cord of DMC pearl cotton along the top edge of the curtain, making ⅛in loops approximately every ⅜-¼in. Before the glue is set run a 1/16in ribbon tape over the cord, butting the edge of the ribbon against the top of the curtain. A spot of extra adhesive may be needed to hold the ribbon in place. When the glue is dry place the curtain in your Pretty Pleater and pleat it (see page 161). Gently remove the fabric from the pleater and hang it on a pole. Glue the pole in place at the window.

Bedding

The single bed in this room is made more comfortable with a mattress, sheets, pillows and blankets. We have three blankets here. Two are quick fabric blankets simply cut to fit and edged with blanket stitch. The other is woven from cream, buff and blue yarn. If you do not have the necessary weaving skills simply omit the woven blanket or make an extra one of the simple fabric blankets (see page 152).

Cotton Mattress

In the early days of Shaker communities mattresses were made of straw but later cotton mattresses were used. These were purchased from dry goods' stores outside the community. Covers made of blue and white cotton ticking were also bought by the sisters, so we made one for the bed here. To make one you will need card, lightweight cotton flannel, blue and white ticking or similar fabric and matching thread.

To make your mattress first measure the size of the

bed inside the frame. It might be useful to cut a card template to the correct size. Use the template as a guide to cut lightweight cotton flannel for the central padding – you will need one piece of fabric three times the width of the bed by its length. Fold it into layers or cut separate sections and stack them to form the pad. Make a cover using blue and white cotton ticking or a similar fabric in the same way as the cover for the mattresses in the Elizabethan bedroom (see page 14) but instead of filling the cover with wool or cotton insert the cotton pad and sew up the end.

BED LINEN

Bed linen was either made of cotton or linen and perfectly plain. The Shaker sisters hand processed flax into linen which was woven into sheets. Cotton sheets, on the other hand, were usually purchased by the bolt and cut into appropriate lengths. Both types were hemmed by hand with a very fine blind stitch.

To make cotton sheets use very fine Egyptian cotton fabric cut into lengths approximately 8½ x 5¾in. Turn tiny double hems, pin with Lills brass pins and hem by hand with a very fine blind stitch such as blind herringbone stitch (see page 160).

PILLOWS AND PILLOWCASES

Shaker pillows were not plump and luxurious but rather meagre in keeping with the austerity of the lifestyle. First make your pillow(s) from fine Egyptian cotton and a filling of cotton wadding, cotton wool or feathers. For the pillowcase(s) you will need the same fine cotton fabric and some fine silk thread, ideally Pearsall's silk gossamer thread.

To make a pillow cut two rectangles of fine cotton fabric 2⅛ x 3⅛in. Place raw edges together and stitch around three sides, taking a ¼in seam allowance. Fill with cotton wadding, cotton wool or feathers, being frugal so that the pillow is not too plump. Turn in the seam allowances along the open edge by ¼in and slipstitch closed.

To make a pillowcase cut a piece of cotton fabric 2¼ x 5⅞in and press it. Now fold under the ends twice by ⅛in, enclosing the raw edge and press flat. Hand stitch with a very fine needle and silk thread. Repeat on the long side edges. When all raw edges are stitched the case should measure 1⅞ x 5½in. Fold one end of the case down by ½in and press, then fold the fabric in half so that both ends meet and press. Open the case and secure the ½in folded flap with a few stitches at the sides. Fold the fabric in half again and blind herringbone stitch the sides closed with fine silk thread.

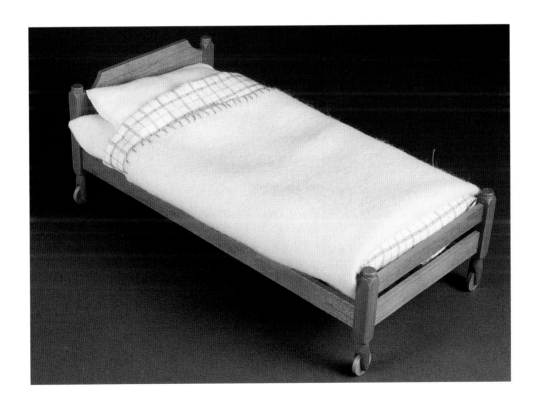

FABRIC BLANKETS

Sometimes bolts of plain woollen cloth were bought and cut up into blankets by the Sisters. The bolts of cloth were almost always in plain woven blue, white or grey with no pattern or adornment. The Sisters would then bind the raw edges with blanket stitch and work initials or numbers in cross stitch in one corner. These marks would identify the owner of the blanket or the room to which items were to be returned after cleaning. They might also be used for alternating the blankets to ensure even wear. Identity marks would not only be stitched on blankets but would also be found on other linens and textiles. The Millennial Laws specified that marking should be done in tiny cross stitches using blue wool or silk thread.

Our room setting features two fabric blankets, one plain and one checked, which are shown in the picture on page 151. Both are easy to make. The plain cream blanket was made from a piece of evenweave, very lightweight wool. To make one simply measure the bed and add extra all round for an overhang then cut your fabric to size. Edge the blanket with tiny blanket stitch. We used matching thread to work the stitch along the long edges but for the visible top edge we used one strand of DMC blue embroidery cotton.

The checked blanket was inspired by the knowledge that sometimes the Sisters would hand weave their own blankets in plain weave or twill variations. Some designs were checks of blue on white. We fashioned the blue and white blanket from a piece of printed checked fabric (similar to the one that we used for the wall cloth).

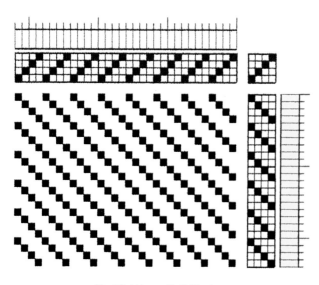

Fig. 50 Woven Twill Blanket

WOVEN TWILL BLANKET

If you have the necessary weaving skills you may like to make this alternative woven blanket for the Shaker bed. It is made to fit a single bed and was designed by Bonni Backe. It is 7½ x 7¼in when finished but weave 8in on the loom for the correct finished length to allow for shrinkage. To make it you will need 30/2 cream-coloured rayon yarn and 30/2 cotton in a natural buff colour and French blue. You will also need a sanding block and No. 120 sandpaper to rough up the nap.

Use 30/2 cream-coloured rayon yarn for the warp. The warp length should be 2yds and the width 8⅜in with a set of 48 epi, reed of 16 dpi and sley of 3 per dent. There should be 410 ends. Use 30/2 cotton for the weft in a natural buff colour and French blue with 42 picks per inch.

Warp the loom as usual. Weave an inch or so header in the tabby, then begin 1/3 twill. Weave following the filling arrangement below and end with 1in of tabby.

Cream: 40 4 4 4 4 4 4 4 4 3⅜in 4 4 4 4 4 4 4 4 4 40

Blue: 2 2 4 2 2 8 2 2 4 2   2 2 2 4 2 2 8 2 2 4 2 2

Cut the finished blanket from the loom and machine stitch at the edge of the twill. Trim to ¼in and unravel to your sewing, being careful not to pull too hard in the last few rows unravelled. Wash in washing-up liquid and water then iron dry. Cover a small block of wood with No. 120 sandpaper. Placing the blanket on a smooth, soft surface, rub the sandpaper across the blanket, first parallel to the stitching and then as the nap develops lengthways on the blanket as well. Only brush the right side to avoid making the blanket too thick.

SHAKER RUG

Although ornamentation was frowned upon, a few warming details were permissible in Shaker interiors including the wall cloth and rugs. This smart woven rug was designed by Bonni Backe and is easy to make if you have weaving skills. If not make a cloth rug by photocopying a design onto fabric as for the wall hangings in the Elizabethan bedroom (see page 21). To make this woven rug you will need 24/2 unbleached cotton, wool or silk such as Jagger Spun Zephyr in indigo, mulberry, ice blue and white or Appleton crewel yarn in similar colours. You

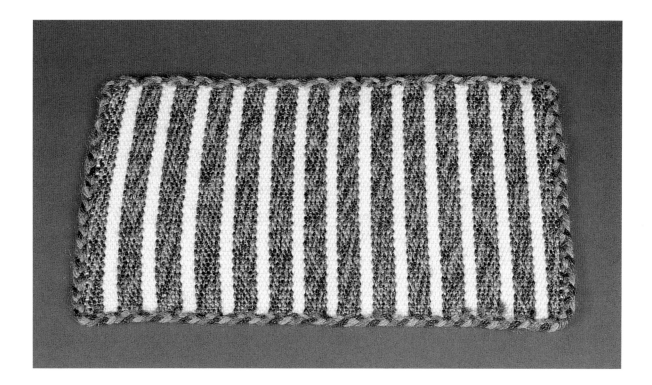

will also need liquid fusible webbing (optional), white glue and invisible nylon sewing thread.

Warp the loom as usual with 24/2 unbleached cotton (approx. 8000 yards per pound). A 2yds warp will weave at least three small Shaker style rugs. There should be 40 picks per inch with 18 ends per inch. Use a wool-silk mix or wool for the weft. The width in the reed should be 3¼in and there should be 58 warp ends.

Make bobbins using two strands of the wool twisted together, one bobbin all white, one bobbin indigo + mulberry and one bobbin indigo + ice blue. Yarns can be twisted by using a bobbin winder or electric drill holding a dowel to wind onto, letting the yarn trail off the end of the bobbin whilst the winder or drill is turning. When the yarn has been twisted sufficiently, bring the yarn to the side to wind onto the bobbin. If flat stick shuttles are used the yarn can be twisted by hand whilst weaving, or twisted using the drill, then wound onto the shuttle.

Using 24/2 cotton, weave ½in firmly beaten header at the beginning of the rug. The wool will also be beaten firmly so it nearly covers the warp. Weave 6 picks of indigo/ice blue, then repeat the following colour sequence until the rug is almost 6in long: indigo/ice blue, 6 picks; indigo/mulberry, 1 pick; white, 6 picks; indigo/mulberry, 1 pick; indigo/ice blue, 8 picks. When the rug measures about 6in, or the desired length (the

finished rug will be 10% shorter than it is now) finish the pattern with indigo/mulberry, 1 pick; white, 6 picks; indigo/mulberry, 1 pick; indigo/ice blue, 6 picks. Weave ½in more of the 24/2 cotton, beating firmly.

Before cutting the weaving from the loom, apply liquid fusible webbing to the cotton headers. When dry, cut off the loom and trim the headers to ¼in. Fold them back and iron them to the back of the rug, following the manufacturer's instructions. If you cannot obtain liquid fusible webbing dilute white glue and apply it to the header. When dry, cut off the loom, trim to ¼in and glue to the back of the rug. Use glue sparingly where the wool begins as you will be sewing the braid on and the glue stiffens the rug.

Braid doubled ends of indigo, ice blue and mulberry to form a strand 20in long. Knot the ends to keep them from unravelling. Beginning at the centre side of the rug, and 1in from the knot in the braid, sew the braid edge to the rug edge, using an overcast stitch and invisible thread. Ease the corners by slightly gathering the braid's inside edge and make small stitches at the corner. When you are within 1½in of the starting point overlap the braid ends and seal the braid with white glue ¼in on each end, beyond where the braids overlap. Leave to dry partially, then continue to sew, tucking the braid ends under so only one layer of braid shows on the front. Steam press.

THE WORKROOM, TOOLS & TECHNIQUES

This chapter contains further information and advice to enable you to complete the projects in this book. However, because of the diversity of projects involved this section cannot be fully comprehensive and a certain amount of basic knowledge is assumed for some of the more specialised techniques such as tatting and weaving. Where this is the case an alternative method of producing a similar item is usually suggested in the project.

PREPARING A WORK AREA

Whether your work space is part of the kitchen table or a whole room keep it clean and tidy and ensure there is plenty of light. For needlework projects there must be sufficient space to follow the job through from planning and design to the administration of final touches before the finished work can be placed in its setting.

FABRICS

It appears that most hobbyists have one or more boxes of saved fabrics both old and new together with assorted sewing threads, embroidery cottons and silks. However, for some of the projects you will also require specific materials such as fine tapestry fabrics. For best results always follow the recommendations with the project. In general we recommend using natural fabrics such as silk, available in various weights, or cotton lawn in plain or patterned colours. These are usually easiest to work with as well as being most authentic, particularly for the historical settings. Heavier upholstery fabrics can be useful if the pattern or weave is fine enough. Look out for old fabrics found in antique shops or flea markets and add these to your fabric box. These work extremely well for dolls' house projects because the colours and feel of an old fabric adds something magical and authentic to a period room setting.

PINS AND NEEDLES

Every work box should have a box of Lills brass pins (14 x .55mm) for quilting and sewing projects because these make pinning small pieces of fabric much easier than with standard dressmakers' pins. Brass lacemaker's pins are also useful for pinning fine fabrics and glass-headed pins are invaluable for pinning out draperies or holding pleats on tablecloths.

A variety of needle sizes is also useful and in particular size 10 or 11 is invaluable for sewing fine fabrics suitable for $\frac{1}{2}$ scale.

THREAD

Ordinary sewing thread is sufficient to work many of the projects in this book, but sometimes it is simply too thick for fine work. Pam Paget-Tomlison of The Linen Press introduced us to Pearsall's silk gossamer threads (available from some fishing tackle shops) and these have not only been added to our work box but we highly recommend them for $\frac{1}{2}$ scale projects. There are seventeen colours in the range with 45 metres on each spool. You will also find that DMC embroidery stranded cottons, stranded silks, hand and machine sewing cottons and Güttermann silk thread come in handy. If you do not have the colour specified in a project you may be able to make do with the colours you do have, but do not be tempted to put economy before quality as otherwise you may be sadly disappointed with your efforts.

WORKROOM TECHNIQUES

There are certain techniques which are needed for the tapestry and embroidery projects in this book. Even if you are already experienced in these fields you will find this information useful because it is specifically aimed at the small-scale work involved here. In particular pay attention to the section on mounting fabric which gives assistance for working tiny pieces.

TRANSFERRING PATTERNS

Needleworkers will know that there are various ways to transfer designs from a pattern to fabric: you can trace it with a soluble pen; use tissue paper and tacking; iron-on transfer pencil; or prick and pounce. Use whichever method you feel happiest with or which best suits the project at hand. Tacking and prick and pounce are the most traditional methods and are explained here.

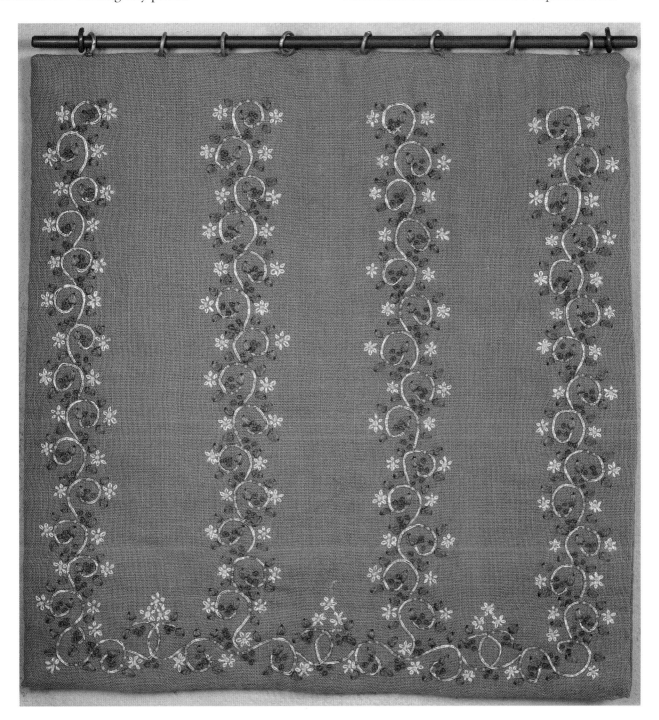

TACKING METHOD

This method is ideal for very pale or delicate fabrics which pen marks might damage or for dark fabrics on which pen marks do not show up. However, on intricate designs you will need to use quite small stitches to ensure that you fully encompass all the details. For this reason it is best to use it only for quite simple designs, otherwise it can be quite time consuming. You may also find that the tacking gets in the way of your embroidery and is difficult to remove afterwards.

Trace your design onto tissue paper. Now work tacking (basting) stitching over the design lines, making sure the stitches are small enough to take in all the details. When all the lines have been outlined carefully remove the tissue paper, leaving the tacking stitches in place. Remove all the tacking lines when the design has been worked.

PRICK AND POUNCE

This somewhat old-fashioned method is particularly useful when working with dark fabrics. The design is transferred to the fabric in a series of dots created by pressing powder through holes in the tracing paper. For large projects it is best to go over the dots with a suitable pen to ensure a more lasting image.

First trace the design onto good-quality tracing paper, then prick along the design lines with a pin or needle – do this over a protected surface to avoid making a series of tiny holes on your work surface. Check that all the lines of the design have been pricked. Now tape your fabric to a firm, flat surface and tape the tracing paper on top. Make a small pad by rolling up a strip of felt and dip it into pounce powder or powdered white chalk. Black pounce is made from finely crushed charcoal, white pounce from cuttlefish and grey pounce is made by mixing the two together. With a circular motion rub the pounce powder very gently over the design. When the design has been covered, carefully lift the corners of the tracing paper to make sure the pattern has been transferred to the fabric. When you are satisfied, remove the tracing and blow to remove excess powder. Then use a fine pencil or paintbrush and appropriate watercolour to fill in the lines.

MOUNTING FABRIC

Even small embroidery and tapestry projects are worth working in a frame or mount to reduce the distortion of the fabric, canvas or gauze. A frame or mount also provides something to hold, making the design easier to work and keeping your hands off the fabric, thereby keeping it cleaner. There are three methods suitable for small projects: using a cardboard mount, fixing the material to muslin and then fitting it in an embroidery hoop or using a flexi-frame. Use the method recommended with the project or whichever you find easiest.

CARDBOARD MOUNT

This method is ideal if you are working a tapestry on silk gauze but it also works well with any small project. Simply measure the finished design and cut a cardboard frame with an opening slightly larger – if it is too neat a fit you will find it awkward to stitch close to the edges. Then simply tape your fabric or gauze to the card, keeping the material as taut as possible and making sure the weave is square with the edges of the card. Mark the top of the mount for reference and if desired mark the centre of the opening along each edge.

EMBROIDERY FRAME

This frame is ideal for working medium to large projects. If you have a large piece of fabric simply mount it in the frame in the usual way. Trapping it between the two hoops and tightening the tension to keep the fabric smooth and taut. Since the fabrics used in this book are quite fine, bind the smaller hoop with cotton tape first, wrapping it over and over the hoop in overlapping strips and stitching the ends together to secure them. Loosen the tension between sewing sessions to avoid marking the fabric. If your fabric is too small to fit into your embroidery frame simply attach it to the centre of a large piece of muslin or fine cotton and then mount the whole piece in the frame.

FLEXI-FRAME

A flexi-frame is a small plastic hoop which is often used as a permanent frame for comparatively small projects. It has two sections, like an embroidery hoop, but there is no tension spring – the hoops fit snugly together and in fact it may take some force to fit the fabric between them. Simply lay the fabric over the inner ring and press the outer ring down hard on top until the two rings snap together.

USING A CHART

Unless you are working a particularly small design it is advisable to stitch tapestry designs from the centre outwards to help minimise distortion of the canvas. The centre row in each direction is marked on the edges of the charts in this book with a black arrow. You need to mark the corresponding central lines on your canvas. To do this fold the canvas in half first vertically and then horizontally and then tack (baste) along the folds with a boldly coloured sewing thread. Mount your fabric in a frame. Find the centre of the chart and thread your needle with the colour nearest to it, using the specified number of strands. Now you can begin. The charts in this book are in colour to help you identify which colour to use. Each square on the chart represents one stitch which is usually worked over one strand of thread in each direction. Work the design in the stitch(es) specified.

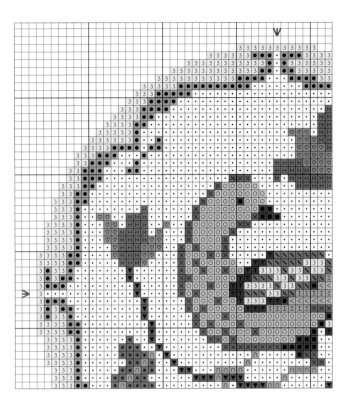

STARTING OFF

There are several methods of starting off a thread. One of the easiest is to start with a waste knot. Simply knot the thread and, starting from the top of the canvas, take your needle down a short distance away from the starting point (about 1–1½in). As your work progresses you will cover the thread at the back of the work and then you can cut off the knot on the front.

Alternatively, begin a short distance away from the starting point and take your thread through from the front to the back of the canvas, leaving a short thread end. Start stitching at the centre of the canvas. After you have worked a row of stitches pull the starting thread to the back of the work, thread it on a needle and thread the yarn through the back of a line of stitches. Trim off the end.

FINISHING OFF

When you have completed a section of stitching with one colour take the needle to the back and thread it through a line of stitches; trim off the loose end. Alternatively, bring the thread up to the front about 1½in away from your last stitch and leave a thread end on the front. Later, when the thread lying across the back of the canvas has been worked over, you can cut off the loose end.

TAPESTRY STITCHES

Needlepoint or tapestry projects are worked in half cross stitch, tent stitch or basketweave. They are all diagonal stitches, worked at a slant across the canvas thread intersections and look the same from the front. For beginners, tent and half cross stitch are easier to manage than basketweave but basketweave causes the least distortion of the canvas so it is particularly effective for background areas and borders. It also pads the back of the canvas well for greater durability.

Left-handers may find it easiest to work the stitches on the opposite diagonal. If you turn the chart upside down and work it that way you will find that the stitches run as normal when it is turned the right way up.

HALF CROSS STITCH

This is the most economical stitch, using the least amount of yarn and it is worked in vertical or horizontal rows. Take care not to pull the yarn too tight. To work the stitch bring the needle up at 1 and go down at 2, up and 3 and down at 4 and so on. When you get to the end of a line you can work back in the opposite direction.

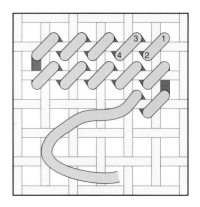

TENT STITCH

Also known as continental stitch, this stitch uses more yarn than half cross stitch for a more stable result. To work the stitch come up at 1 and go down at 2, up at 3 and down at 4 and so on. Work from right to left. When you reach the end of a row thread the needle through the back of previously worked stitches to the start of the next row.

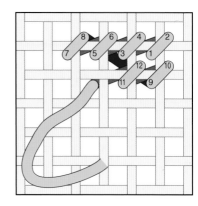

BASKETWEAVE STITCH

This stitch hardly distorts the canvas at all and is worked on the diagonal. Basketweave stitch uses the most yarn but this helps pad the work and make it durable. To work the stitch bring the needle up at 1, go down at 2, up at 3 and down at 4. Now come up at 5, go down at 6, up at 7 and down at 8. Next come up at 9, go down at 10, up at 11 and down at 12. From now on you can continue working on the diagonal.

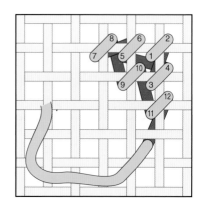

EMBROIDERY STITCHES

Here are instructions for working the stitches used in this book. However, many of the embroidery projects can be worked in whatever stitches you feel most comfortable with, so feel free to use your imagination and creative talents.

BACKSTITCH

This stitch is used for sewing seams and outlining design areas in embroideries. Bring the needle up at the start of the sewing line at 1. Take it down at 2 and bring it up at 3 a little further along. Now take the needle back down at 2 and bring it up at 4. Continue in this way to work along the required line.

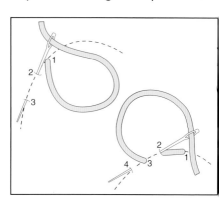

WHIPPED BACKSTITCH

This is a decorated backstitch which is useful where a fancy outline is required. First work a line of backstitch. Using the same or a contrasting colour bring your whipping thread up close to the first backstitch. Switch to a tapestry needle and pass the thread under the first backstitch, then come back under the second stitch in the opposite direction. Continue along the line in the same way.

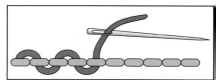

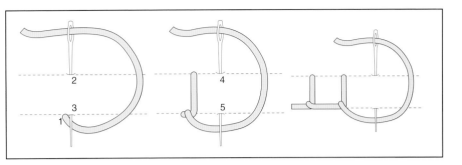

BLANKET STITCH (above)

This is used to finish raw edges or worked as a decorative stitch in the middle of a fabric. Bring the needle up at 1. Go down at 2 and come up at 3, passing the thread under the needle. Repeat. When finishing a fabric edge, 2 should go under the fabric edge.

CHAIN STITCH

Bring your needle up at 1. Go down at 2 then bring the needle up at 3, catching the working thread. Form the thread into a neat loop and then repeat. Catch down the last stitch with a small straight stitch in the same way as for Lazy Daisy Stitch (page 160).

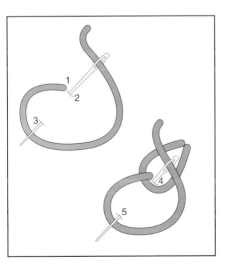

COUCHING

Bring the decorative thread up on the right side of the fabric at the start of the design line. Take it back down at the end of the line or work in short sections if preferred. Using a finer thread bring the needle up next to the decorative thread at 1 and take it down on the opposite side at 2. Make your next stitch about ⅛-¼in further on.

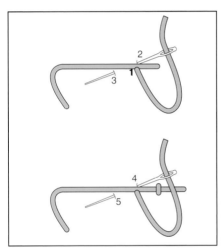

CROSS STITCH

Work this stitch in an imaginary square. Bring the needle up at the bottom left of your 'square' at 1. Take the needle down at the top right at 2 and bring it up at the bottom right at 3. To finish the stitch take it back down at the top left at 4.

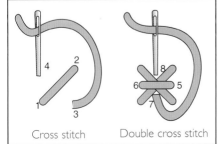

Cross stitch   Double cross stitch

DOUBLE CROSS STITCH (STAR STITCH)

First work a cross stitch (see bottom left). Now bring your needle up on the right at 5, midway between 2 and 3). Take the needle down on the left at 6 and bring it up at the bottom at 7. Finally, take the needle down at the centre top at 8 to finish.

FEATHER STITCH

Bring the needle up at 1. Take it down at 2 and bring it up halfway between the two and lower down at 3, looping the thread under the needle. Now go down at 4 and come up at 5, again looping the thread under. Repeat to fill the required area.

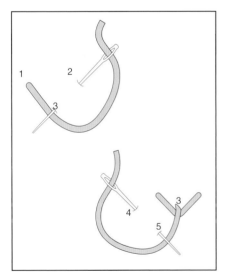

FRENCH KNOT

Bring the needle up at 1, wrap the working thread once or twice around it and push the thread down. Take the needle down close to 1 at 2, pulling the thread through.

LAZY DAISY STITCH (DETACHED CHAIN STITCH)

Bring the needle up at 1. Go down at 2 and then bring the needle up at 3, catching the working thread. Form the thread into a neat loop and then take a small stitch over it.

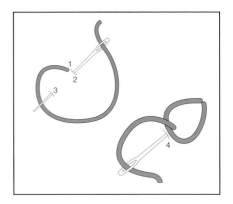

SATIN STITCH

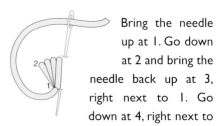

Bring the needle up at 1. Go down at 2 and bring the needle back up at 3, right next to 1. Go down at 4, right next to 2, and then bring the needle back up at 5, right next to 3. Continue in this way until the whole area is covered. Stitches can be angled as necessary.

STEM STITCH

Bring the needle up at 1. Go down at 2 and bring it up at 3, above the working thread and halfway between 1 and 2. Keep the working thread under the needle.

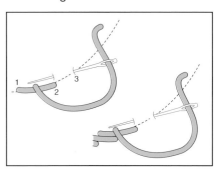

SEWING STITCHES

There are a few basic sewing stitches you need to know in order to complete some of the soft furnishings in this book. In addition to standard running stitch these comprise whipstitch, slipstitch and blind herringbone stitch. We recommend that you use very fine thread for sewing miniature projects, such as Pearsall's silk gossamer thread which is more in keeping with the scale of dolls' house furnishings (see thread, page 154).

BLIND HERRINGBONE STITCH

This is a professional hemming stitch. Fold the edge of the fabric back so that the stitches are invisible in the final item. Working from left to right, bring the needle up and take a small backstitch on the main fabric (1). Move the needle to the right and take a small backstitch on the fold of the hem at 2. Continue in this way to the end.

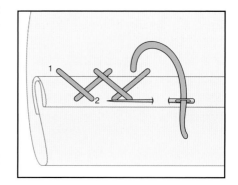

SLIPSTITCH (shown top right)

Use this strong stitch to finish hems or to close the opening between two edges. Working from right to left, bring the needle up on one side at 1 and insert it in the other side ⅟₁₆in further along at 2. Bring the needle out a short distance along at 3 and then cross to

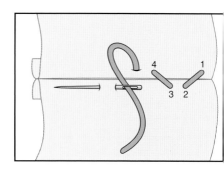

the other side again ⅟₁₆in further along at 4 to catch a short piece of fabric. Continue in this way to the end.

RUNNING STITCH

This is the simplest stitch of all to work and is used in this book to join two fabric layers together. Simply bring the needle up at the start of the stitching line at 1. Go down at 2 and come up at 3, one stitch length further on. Repeat to work the whole line.

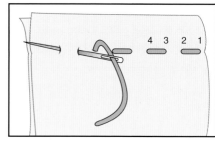

WHIPSTITCH

This simple stitch is very quick to work and is used to join two edges together in the same way as slipstitch. Simply bring the needle up on one side at 1 and insert it on the other side at 2, bringing it up again at 3 a little way beyond 1. Continue in this way to the end.

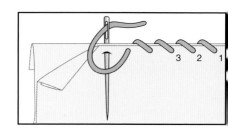

BLOCKING CANVAS

Blocking is not generally needed for small projects, but it may be necessary for some of the larger items. You will need a soft board such as chipboard, dressmakers' squared paper, masking tape, nails and a hammer.

Simply centre the dressmakers' paper on your board and tape it down. Dampen your needlework evenly and lay it on top, aligning one corner with a square on the paper. Nail in place. Aligning one edge with a line on the paper and starting from the nailed corner, nail one side of the needlework to the board, inserting a nail on every other line. Repeat to nail the adjacent side. Work out where the free corner will go and nail in place, then complete nailing the remaining sides. As the needlework dries the creases and wrinkles will ease out. Leave to dry completely before removing the needlework.

USING A PRETTY PLEATER

A Pretty Pleater is used extensively in this book for gathering fabrics, especially for curtains. It is easy to use on all sorts of fabrics including sheers, ribbons, lace and ordinary dressmaking or fine upholstery fabrics. However, in general the manufacturer recommends using fabrics with natural fibres on the basis that 'fabric that wrinkles easily usually pleats easily.'

A Pretty Pleater comprises a metal tray with a series of parallel slots or grooves in it. All you do is lay your fabric over the top and use the card provided to press the fabric into the first groove. Still holding the fabric in the first groove, press it into the next groove. Work your way along the fabric in this way, always holding the fabric in place in the previous groove. To help the pleats cling to the grooves, iron the fabric as you go. Spray starch will help to hold the pleats in place when you have finished.

BINDING AN EDGE

This technique is used to finish the edges of quilts or for binding rugs. First decide on the width of binding which you require – ¼in should be fine unless you want a wider border. Multiply this by two and add ½in for seam allowances – 1in. Measure the two long edges of the item to be bound and cut out two strips your calculated width (1in) by the length. Stitch one long edge of a binding strip to each long edge of the item with right sides facing and taking a ¼in seam allowance. Fold the fabric strip over to the back of the item and tuck in the raw edges by ¼in. Slipstitch in place. Now measure the short edges of the item, including the binding, and cut two more strips, this time adding ½in to the length. Attach them in the same way, enclosing the raw ends of the first binding strips and tucking in the raw ends of these strips too.

ATTACHING A LINING

Sometimes you will wish to line items for greater durability, such as the tapestry rugs or bed covers. Here is the simplest method of doing this.

Trim the item to size, leaving a small seam allowance of ¼–½in all round and measure it. Fold under the seam allowances on all sides and press. Now cut a piece of lining fabric to your measurements and trim off about ⅛–¼in all round. Press under the same seam allowance as you used on the main item. With wrong sides facing pin your two pieces together and slipstitch all round the edges. Your lining will be slightly smaller than the main piece, ensuring that it doesn't show on the right side. Press the finished item.

MAKING A SIMPLE LOOM

Ina Wichers has kindly provided these instructions for making a loom which will enable you to weave the woven rug in the Larsson room and other rag rugs for your dolls' house. You will need an artist's canvas stretcher or picture frame, small nails and a hammer, a sheet of graph paper, glue, a tape measure and strips of thin wood or thick cardboard to make a few shuttles and a shed stick. You will also need some strong linen or firm cotton

thread for the warp and finely woven cloth such as light-weight cotton lawn for the weft.

Check that your frame is square and sand it lightly to remove any rough areas, if necessary. Place the frame on a flat surface and glue a piece of graph paper to both short sides, so both pieces are placed the same way. Draw dots as a guide for the nails in two staggered rows as shown in Fig. 51. Ina positioned four nails per inch to give eight threads per inch but this can be adjusted to suit the thickness of the thread and cloth strips. Hammer the nails in well at the marked positions.

Fig. 51 Nailing Guide

Cut a shuttle for each colour to be woven from thick card or thin wood using the pattern in Fig. 52. If you are using wood make sure the ends are very smooth and that the wood is very thin to avoid tearing the threads. Make a shed stick to pass between the warp threads so that when it is lifted every second thread is raised up and the shuttle can be passed through. Make the shed stick from a straight piece of wood which is wider than the loom, again making sure it is very smooth.

Fig. 52 Shuttle Pattern

SHUTTLE

RESOURCES AND ADDRESS BOOK

SILK THREADS AND EMBROIDERY SILKS

Mulberry Silks
2 Old Rectory Cottages
Easton Grey
Malmesbury
Wiltshire SN16 0PE

For Pearsall's Silk Gossamer Thread by Mail Order
Tom C. Saville Ltd
9 Notting Road
Trowell
Nottingham NG9 3PA
(Tel: 0115-930-8800)

YARNS FOR WEAVING

For Appleton yarns (Shaker rug)
Appleton Bros Ltd
Thames Works
Church Street
Chiswick
London W4 2PE
(Tel: 020-8994-0711)
(Fax: 020-8995-06609)

For 24/2 unbleached cotton (Shaker rug)
C. L. Blomqvist
Box 111
SE-510 20 Fritsla, Sweden
http://www.c.b.se
e-mail: blomqvist@swipnet.se

For Jagger Spun Yarn (Shaker rug)
The Knitters Underground/
The Weaver's Loft
308 S. Pennsylvania Avenue
Centre Hall
PA 16828   USA
e-mail: yarnshop@aol.com

For 60/2 cotton, natural
Weevings
c/o Bonni Backe
203 London Road,
Apt 607
Concord
NH 03301, USA
e-mail: weevings@juno.com
http://weavings.com

FABRICS AND HABERDASHERY

The Dolls' House Draper
P.O. Box 128
Lightcliffe
Halifax
W. Yorkshire HX3 8RN

Fabric for Caren Garfen samplers
Elizabeth R. Anderson
'Miniature Embroideries'
Rosedale
Tall Elm Close
Bromley,
Kent BR2 0TT

The Silk Route
32 Wolseley Road
Godalming
Surrey GU7 3EA

ARTISANS AND NEEDLEWORKERS

Anglesey Dolls Houses
5a Penrhos Industrial Estate
Holyhead
Anglesey
LL65 2UQ

Bonni Backe
(see Weevings)

Fiona Bailey
c/o Miniature Needlework
Society, UK

Sue Bakker
13 Drovers Way
Peebles
Scotland EH45 9BN

Jill Bennett
Mendip Lodge
8 Bathwick Hill
Bath BA2 6EW

David Booth
18 Narrabeen Road
Cheriton
Folkestone
Kent CT19 4DD

Tom Burchmore
Unit D 12A
Dower House Farm
Workshop
Blackboys
Uckfield
East Sussex BN27 4DZ

C. & J. Gallery
109 S. Elmwood
Suite 18
Oak Park
IL 60302, USA

James Carrington
8 Cheriton Square
London SW17 8AE

Sue Cook
Unit 5, Arundel Mews
Arundel Place
Brighton
East Sussex BN2 1GD

Country Comforts
The Chapel

Church Place
Pulborough
West Sussex RH20 1AF

Crochet by Yvonne
1 Duffield Cottage
Duffield Lane
Newborough
Burton-on-Trent
Staffordshire DE13 8SH

Divers Workes
21 Cranberry Way
Hull
E Yorkshire HU4 7AG

Edwardian Elegance
48 Chapel Lane
Wilmslow
Cheshire SK9 5HZ

E.L.F. Kitchens
101 Glenville Grove
London SE8 4BJ

Annelle Fergusson
(c/o Miniature Needlework
Society, UK)

Sheila Grantham
(c/o Miniature Needlework
Society, UK)

John J. Hodgson
Colston Grange
25 Sands Lane
Bridlington
E Yorkshire YO15 2JG

Yvonne Hodson
(see Crochet by Yvonne)

Charlotte Hunt
31 Westover Road
London SW18 2RE

David Hurley
52 Nicholas Mead
Great Linford
Milton Keynes
Buckinghamshire MK14 5EL

Lynne Johnson
2 Fairfield Close
Staveley, Kendal
Cumbria LA8 9RA

Tony Knott
Chapet House
Chipping Norton
Oxfordshire OX7 5SZ

Alison Larkin
(see Divers Workes)

The Linen Press
Easton House
Easton, Wells
Somerset BA5 1EF

Nicola Mascall
8 Horton Street
Frome
Somerset BA11 3DP

Ann Miller
(c/o Miniature Needlework
    Society, USA)

**Miniature Needlework
    Society**
c/o Annelle Fergusson
111 Gibbs Ferry Lane
Clinton TN 37716 USA

**Miniature Needlework
    Society**
c/o Jill Swift
The Spinney
Holm next the Sea
Norfolk PE36 6LF

Clare Minty
23 St James Road
Hereford HR1 2QS

Pam Paget-Tomlison
(see The Linen Press)

Lynne Parkinson
(see Peppermint Designs)

Pear Tree Miniatures
The Pear Tree
Eglwyswrw
Pembrokeshire SA41 3UP

Peppermint Designs
Peppermint Hall
The Still Leverington
Wisbech Cambs PE13 5DQ

Petite Fleur
Appleton Wiske
Northallerton
N Yorkshire DL8 2AA

Gill Rawling
(see Petite Fleur)

d. Anne Ruff Miniatures
1100 Vagabond Lane
Plymouth

MN 55447   USA
e-mail:
    Rruff68098@aol.com

Kim Selwood
Springbank
75 James Street
Hellensburgh
Scotland G84 8XH

Georgina Steeds
85 Summerleaze Road
Maidenhead
Berkshire SL6 8ER

Stokesay Ware
37 Sandbrook Road
Stoke Newington
London N16 0SH

Raymond Storey
The Willows
59 Park Crescent
Shiremoor
Newcastle-upon-Tyne
NE27 0LJ

Terence Stringer
Spindles
Lexham Road
Litcham
Norfolk PE32 2QQ

Tarbena Miniatures
Garden Cottage
Bardfield Road
Shalford
Essex CM7 5HX

Phyllis Tucker
5748 Southbridge Lane
Columbus
OH 43213, USA

Rosalene Walters
(c/o Miniature Needlework
    Society, UK)

Ray Whitledge
3910 King Arthur Road
Annadale
VA 22003 USA
e-mail: RWmin@aol.com

Ina Wichers
(see Country Comforts)

DOLLS' HOUSE
PUBLICATIONS
AND GUILDS

**International Dolls'
    House News**
Ashdown.co. uk
Avalon Court
Star Road
Partridge Green
Sussex RH13 8RY

**International Guild of
    Miniature Artisans**
c/o Annelle Fergusson
111 Gibbs Ferry Lane
Clinton TN 37716, USA

ACKNOWLEDGEMENTS

We should like to express our extreme gratitude to Sally Howard-Smith and Annelle Fergusson, co-ordinators of the Miniature Needlework Society in England and America, respectively, whose introduction to several of their members resulted in a number of the projects in this book. We are particularly thankful to Sue Bakker, Bonni Backe, Fiona Bailey, Caren Garfen, Sheila Grantham, Annelle Fergusson, Yvonne Hodson, Lynne Johnson, Alison Larkin, Dora Lockyer, Ann Miller, Clare Minty, Pam Paget-Tomlison, Jill Swift and Rosalene Walters.

We should also like to thank the following for lending items for use in our room settings: David Hurley, C & J Gallery, Edwardian Elegance, E.L.F. Kitchens, The Linen Press, Pear Tree Miniatures, Tarbena Miniatures, Jill Bennett, David and Dulcie Booth, Tom Burchmore, James Carrington, Charlotte Hunt, John Hodgson, Tony Knott, Gill Rawling, John Roebuck, d. Anne Ruff, Kim Selwood, Georgina Steeds, Terence Stringer, Stokesay Ware, Raymond Storey, Phyllis Tucker, Ray Whitledge and Ina Wichers.

INDEX

A DAVID & CHARLES BOOK

Photography by Nick Forder

First published in the UK in 2001

Text and designs Copyright © Nick and Esther Forder 2001
Photography and layout Copyright © David & Charles 2001

Nick & Esther Forder have asserted their right to be identified as authors of this work in accordance with the Copyright, Designs and Patents Act, 1988.

A catalogue record for this book is available from the British Library.

ISBN 0 7153 0979 X

Page layout by Visual Image
Printed in Hong Kong by Dai Nippon
for David & Charles
Brunel House   Newton Abbot   Devon